"Using the ancient text of the Apostles' Creed as a framework, Dinter offers a provocative and accessible exploration for those seeking to reflect on what it means to be a Christian believer in the twenty-first century."

—Kevin Ahern, Manhattan College

"*This I Believe* is a sensationally refreshing approach to the New Testament, both accurate and personal, historical and contemporary. The reader finds himself in such capable hands, exploring the deeper meanings of the Christian Bible."

—Thomas Cahill, author of *Hinges of History*

"At this time when social justice Catholicism is often under attack—even from some members of the episcopate—Paul Dinter's book is an important reminder that a faith that does justice is central not just to evangelization, but also to the very understanding of the Credo and of Christ's paschal mystery."

—Massimo Faggioli, Villanova University

"Faith communities have been vital in the efforts to implement restorative justice through education, arts programming, and musical programs. *This I Believe* demonstrates the critical connections between religious faith and justice efforts that I have continually witnessed in my own work. In over twenty years in the social justice field, one thing has always been clear: religious volunteers never give up on the people they serve. This important book shows how these worlds collide in lifesaving ways."

—Sean Pica, executive director,
  Hudson Link for Higher Education in Prison

This I Believe

A FAITH THAT DOES JUSTICE

This I Believe

A FAITH THAT DOES JUSTICE

"... *seek ye first the Kingdom of God and its justice* ..."

Paul E. Dinter

FOREWORD BY
Joseph J. Fahey

CASCADE *Books* • Eugene, Oregon

THIS I BELIEVE
A Faith That Does Justice

Copyright © 2022 Paul E. Dinter. All rights reserved. Except for brief quotations in critical publications or reviews, no part of this book may be reproduced in any manner without prior written permission from the publisher. Write: Permissions, Wipf and Stock Publishers, 199 W. 8th Ave., Suite 3, Eugene, OR 97401.

Cascade Books
An Imprint of Wipf and Stock Publishers
199 W. 8th Ave., Suite 3
Eugene, OR 97401

www.wipfandstock.com

PAPERBACK ISBN: 978-1-6667-3507-9
HARDCOVER ISBN: 978-1-6667-9175-4
EBOOK ISBN: 978-1-6667-9176-1

Cataloguing-in-Publication data:

Names: Dinter, Paul E., author. | Joseph J. Fahey, foreword.

Title: This I believe : a faith that does justice / Paul E. Dinter.

Description: Eugene, OR: Cascade Books, 2022 | Includes bibliographical references.

Identifiers: ISBN 978-1-6667-3507-9 (paperback) | ISBN 978-1-6667-9175-4 (hardcover) | ISBN 978-1-6667-9176-1 (ebook)

Subjects: LCSH: Bible—Hermeneutics. | Bible—Language, style. | Faith and reason.

Classification: BR124 D50 2022 (print) | BR124 (ebook)

All translations, when not the author's own, are taken from the New Revised Standard Version, New York: Oxford University Press, 1991.

To Marilyn
Partner, Rescuer, Spouse

Table of Contents

Foreword | *Joseph J. Fahey* | xi
Introduction | xv
Chapter 1: The Language of Faith and Its Perils | 1
Chapter 2: The Origin Stories of Jesus of Nazareth | 5
Chapter 3: Extending the Narrative: The Apostles' Creed | 17
    i. God: Creator and Triune | 20
    ii. Born of the Virgin Mary | 30
    iii. Descended into hell | 36
    iv. Rose again | 37
    v. Ascended into heaven | 40
    vi. Sits at the right hand of God | 43
    vii. To judge the living and the dead | 45
        Doing Justice Today | 51
            Racial justice
            Economic and social justice
            Ecological/environmental justice
            Restorative justice
            Gender justice
            Sexual justice
            Reproductive justice
    viii. The Holy Spirit | 71
    ix. The holy catholic church | 73
    x. The communion of saints | 83
    xi. The forgiveness of sins | 87

TABLE OF CONTENTS

xii. The resurrection of the dead, and the life of the world-to-come | 90

Chapter 4: Faith as Doing Justice | 103

Appendix A | 107

Bibliography | 115

Foreword

Joseph J. Fahey

THOSE OF US RAISED in the Roman Catholic tradition in the 1940s and 1950s were repeatedly told that our goal in life was to "save our souls" from this "vale of tears" that was our human existence. To do this, we needed to renounce the devil and engage in daily combat with demonic temptations of the "sins of the flesh" that would keep us from heaven after death. The Catholic Church trained its priests primarily to administer the sacraments that provided divine grace necessary to save our souls from the wiles of the devil. Salvation for us meant leaving this earthly "world of sin" for happiness in an afterlife that was the "kingdom of heaven."

This wonderful book by an old friend and colleague, Paul Dinter, persuasively challenges that worldview and urges us to understand that our mission is to seek the reign of God in *this life* through the establishment of justice here on earth. In Dr. Dinter's words, "In my understanding, questions of justice hold first place in any adequate reckoning between faith and humanity's tenuous fate. For too long, religious commitment and sentiment have skirted the demands of justice as an add-on, not as central to faith." Dr. Dinter understands justice in a biblical, rather than legal, sense to mean, "The Lord whose joy it is to lift up the poor, raise the lowly to high places, free the captives, and announce the good news of the Jubilee..."

Foreword

We are then led though a journey that demythologizes much of the story of the origin of Jesus of Nazareth through a rigorous examination of the myths, symbols, and metaphors upon which the Jesus narrative is founded. Quite clearly Dr. Dinter has mastered volumes of biblical scholarship that seek to understand Jesus in the context of the historical events of his time, along with the myths attendant to it. Of particular interest is the discussion of the "virgin birth" and the role of Mary in the mission of Jesus. Quite clearly, Mary's "Magnificat" is foundational to the social justice mission of Jesus.

The heart of this book is Dr. Dinter's discussion of the ancient Apostles' Creed and the centrality that justice plays in each of the creed's teachings, from "I believe in God the Father Almighty . . ." to ". . . the resurrection of the body, and the life of the world to come. Amen." Throughout this lucid and learned discussion, Dr. Dinter helps us to understand that the Apostles' Creed is as much an ethical document as it is a statement of faith. Indeed, the Creed is rooted in the conviction of the Hebrew prophets that "justice names the heart of the divine/human relationship."

Dr. Dinter specifically discusses seven categories of justice: racial, economic/social, ecological/environmental, restorative, gender, sexual, and reproductive justice. He links each category to the Creed in a way that is quite challenging to traditional norms that isolate ethical teaching from a faith based on justice and love. Dr. Dinter does not shy away from controversial interpretations of the seven categories of justice. Those who hold orthodox views on these categories will find Dinter's insights both challenging and provocative. Let them challenge you!

A highlight of this entire discussion is the "forgiveness of sins," where Dr. Dinter reminds us of the teaching of Jesus about reconciliation: "So if you are offering your gift at the altar, and there remember that your brother has something against you, leave your gift there before the altar and go; first to be reconciled to your brother, and then come and offer your gift" (Matt 5:23–24) Here, Jesus is explicitly telling us that moral acts of establishing just relationships between people are more important than worship itself.

Foreword

Indeed, there can be no authentic ritual worship or statement of faith that is not rooted in justice. That is the core of this book.

Dr. Dinter succinctly sums up the message of this book with the following statement that invites all of us to thoroughly reexamine our previous convictions about the relationship between statements of belief and the work of justice: "The narrative embedded in the Creed captures a much larger, more cosmic tale of Love as the beginning and end of all things beyond suffering and death. But the ultimate and ever-present correlate of that Love resides in God's Justice. Enacted by repentance, and carried out via mercy, forgiveness and reconciliation, this justice is the highest calling of all who make the Creed their own."

In conclusion, I should like to say a word about my relationship with Paul Dinter as I have known him. I first met Paul in the 1970s when he was a young priest who served as the Catholic chaplain at Columbia University in New York City. At the time, I taught theology at Manhattan College and served as General Secretary of Pax Christi, USA, the international Catholic peace movement. Paul invited me to give a lecture at Columbia and from that moment we became close friends and longtime collaborators in the cause of peace through justice. Paul taught at Manhattan College for many years and, since we shared an office, we engaged in many conversations on the urgent topics of the day.

In Paul Dinter I met a disciplined but playful mind who sought always—in John Henry Newman's words—"to map out the universe." And, in Paul, I met a heart full of love and compassion for those in prison and those who are spiritually imprisoned.

You too, dear reader, will meet Paul Dinter in the inspiring pages that follow. Let us together labor for justice here on earth that is the essence of the reign of God.

Joseph J. Fahey was a professor of religious studies at Manhattan College for fifty years. He is the author of *War and the Christian Conscience* (Orbis).

Introduction

CHRISTMAS 2020 SURVIVED COVID-19. But not without the pandemic inflicting great pain and suffering. For myself, questions about "why" and "for what" haunted the feast, its resonance and its truth. How could we be singing "Silent Night" when, down the street, an emergency room overflowed with gurneys and their ventilated patients? The very collision of the two wore on me and prompted me to spend some time revisiting Christianity's ancient narrative. Would its "good news" stand up to scrutiny if I looked deeply into it? Since then, COVID has kept taking victims, a surrogate for many unseen perils confronting humanity. Alongside so many human-induced disasters, wars, and conflicts, the pandemic has forced me to dig deeper into "the reason concerning the hope we have" (1 Pet 3:15) that I see hiding below the surface of this age-old narrative. Allow me, then, to revisit December's strange but familiar story to start with. I will then move on to look at the stranger beliefs appearing in the longer narrative known as the Apostles' Creed. Within this search, I hope finally to lay out some of the challenges/promises latent in the larger Christian narrative of salvation as the international community moves deeper into this perilous century.

What can the full story really offer churchgoers, seekers, or even skeptics? Can I reach the unaffiliated, growing cadre of millennials styling themselves Nones? What about all kinds of folks searching to get some purchase on their place in the cosmos today? In short, can I uncover a disguised vitality within the overall

INTRODUCTION

narrative that can resolve seeming contradictions between ancient forms and contemporary meaning? I'm willing to try, but I need to confess something up front. To my mind, questions of justice hold first place today in any adequate reckoning between religious faith and humanity's tenuous fate. For too long, religious commitment and sentiment of all sorts have skirted the demands of justice, seeing them as an add-on, not as central to faith.

But as the pandemic and our tragic responses have made clear, the human playing field is not a level one. Millions continue to suffer from the injustices around profound inequity in both life resources and life-saving care. Clearly, viruses long predate the Gospels and the Creed. But today they are only one of the natural world's voices calling humanity to answer the call to "repent and believe," to change our way of thinking about the human story itself. In its own way, the convergence of this virulent coronavirus and the story behind Christmas has the power to redefine what Christian faith has to say for itself and how believers should act upon it.

Perched as I am well into my eighth decade, I began to wrestle with the challenges, the temptations, and the beauty found in the fullness of the Christ story back in my seminary days. In short order, I was ministering as a chaplain on a large secular campus. Preaching there made wonderful demands on me, as did my work among scientists and humanists challenging the nuclear buildup of the 1980s, local homelessness, and even urban poverty. Personally, my vantage point has always begun in Roman Catholicism, but it extends much further than matters only Christians must attend to. This, despite the Christian story's clumsy unfolding over two millennia that has come to define "church" for many people today. I can't dispute that.

But I am undertaking this quest as a record of my own story: from youthful belief, through critical investigating, to living beyond ordained ministry, to surviving as a "recovered" Catholic Christian. My journey has involved decades of studying, thinking, weathering crises, not a little prayer, but also some deep discoveries as well. Some of my formulations of the story's mythic and

INTRODUCTION

symbolic power will resonate with many churchgoers. But others may well prove a scandal. None of them have been arrived at lightly or dispassionately. Together they seek to open a way through the sea of doubt and disbelief that have left too many unmoored from faith affiliation in any meaningful way. People of good will abound, but many would-be believers are fending for themselves in our current social, economic, and political morass. I write, then, for them as well as for myself and any legacy these thoughts might engender.

CHAPTER 1

The Language of Faith and Its Perils

In which I seek to explain how not to understand symbolic stories whose literal truth claims too easily undermine the underlying truth value of the entire biblical narrative.

MY QUEST STARTS WITH a note about language and its ambiguous role in faith expression—its value, but also its insufficiency. Words in narrative form remain a central conduit for our telling stories. Arising from mental images, they emerge into striking visual and artistic panoramas and become narratives—of the cosmos, humanity, Christ, the church, ourselves. As stories, they have given people from time immemorial a way to make sense of things. Stories long predated philosophy, doctrines, scientific hypotheses, or any proofs and formulas that have today helped us know our place in the physical universe. But neither scientific knowledge, nor our image-filled narratives, can "tell the whole story." We must trade in both when we seek any larger truth to guide us along our journey through this life.

Still, the language of story that I will examine here lays traps along the way. Words shoulder many levels of meaning. Gathered into stories, they expand our imaginative horizons. Alternately, they can shrink a narrative's compass into its first reading, so to speak, locking it in as the (one and only) meaning. We call this literalism. I will argue that it unknowingly carries with it the death of religious truth. In the pre-modern world of interpreting ancient texts like the Bible's many books, the "literal" level merely laid the foundation from which sprang deeper poetic, moral, and spiritual riches. The rabbis knew that long before Christian writers tried to work out various levels of meaning in the canonical texts. But this art fell by the wayside more recently with the impetus for pinning down the *bruta facta* of history and nature. The modern search for *facts* yielded both a new language anchored in reason and, eventually, scientific knowledge. Words began to be measured for their demonstrable weight. Language, from the Western Renaissance to the present, tends toward privileging literal definitions, testing propositions, falsifying meanings, and leaving the discarded behind. In its basest forms it becomes data to be aggregated and marketed!

Christian storytelling, often seen as opposing reason and science, ironically followed suit. For most Protestants, the literal meaning of stories became the criterion for their religious truth. For their part, Catholics turned away from the biblical canon's comfort with ambiguity. Church teachers preferred reasoned "proofs" as the surer road to faith's truth claims. Even today, these warring certitudes wear away at the poetic strength of the language of faith. For both groups, only doctrinaire religion could challenge doctrinaire science. As dueling fundamentalisms, they have cramped the spiritual riches of the narratives and the traditions sprung from them. Often alone, poets and artists have moved above this wasteland to celebrate the expansive meanings that a living tradition needs to breathe and live.

For their part, the best preachers intuit how to recast stories in ways that grab their listeners and move them. In the years I was able to exercise that ministry, I approached the task with the proverbial "fear and trembling," but I also delighted in finding new voices speaking out of old texts: recasting the ministry of Jesus, seeing him as the ultimate advance man for God's kingdom, or retelling his encounter with "the woman at the well of desire." Deconstructing "kingship" in terms of servant leadership, rediscovering anti-racism in simple parables, upending economic realities about the need to "pay the price," raising the "cup of thanksgiving" as a sacramental act that frees us from resentment, or undoing notions of guilt by discovering unexpected places where "grace abounds"—these all flowed from my efforts to pour new wine into new wineskins. I may have not been the best vintner, but I always sought to make the most of the harvest such as I saw it.

All these efforts flowed from my conviction that rigid orthodoxies deprive religious beliefs of their beauty as well as their goodness and truth. Left bleeding on the side of the road, as well, lies their comedic power. For comedy, or the reversal of grim fates and circumstances, lies at the heart of the biblical tradition. And biblical comedy shows itself as *non-tragedy* chiefly in the pursuit and practice of justice. In biblical narratives, comedy intrudes in the form of topsy-turvy outcomes, unlikely life strategies, and all sorts of foolish actors and actions. It turns out that, in the New Testament, attention to God's way of being just upends the "virtue" of justice in much the same way that it confounds common notions about religious activity. For believers, Ultimate Truth, the realm of the divine (also called Transcendence), reveals itself even in the doleful events burdening our passage through this world. The best response to the deeply tragic view of life and of the entire cosmos, so *au courant* today, remains justice. The Lord's joy in lifting up the poor, raising the lowly to high places, freeing the captives, and announcing the good news of the Jubilee Year of liberation inspired these old narratives. A lively conviction about how we also can do justice can answer many of the challenges society faces to this day.

So I see the biblical revelation, and the viable faith structures built upon it, as far more than "mere" stories. Of old, the Torah and Talmud of Judaism constructed a mighty edifice for religious and social life, expanding on the narratives and laws of the Tanach (the Hebrew Bible). So too the Christian Scriptures, and the earliest writings and practices based on them, contain moral and legal prescriptions. But, like the rabbis' expansive storytelling collected in the Midrashim ("searches" for deeper meaning in the ancient

This I Believe

texts[1]), the best Christian storytellers engage in text-mining, digging into myth and symbolic speech to uncover life-giving truths. Yet when the early church began to thread its narrative of "lifting up the lowly to high places" through ancient philosophic lenses, a shift began to occur. Taken hostage as well by imperial politics (which have survived in one form or another into the twenty-first century), the story experienced increasing difficulty witnessing to the "good news" about the scandal of Divine Love. Philosophical reasoning, legalistic morality, and didactic instruction often consign mystery to a black hole where little of it survives. When this happens, we are left with ideologies, cramped systems of requirement and reward. God's death inevitably follows.

In this, my testimony of belief, I begin by looking specifically at "the Christmas story" as a test case about what believers are committing themselves to when they retell it. After trying to spell out some contemporary meaning in these long-ago events, I will push the inquiry further to the larger narrative captured in the Apostles' Creed. This early profession of faith tells a story whose universal scope still possesses truth value for our technologically evolved age.[2] Seeking to uncover its underlying comforts and challenges for religious seekers, I will venture to interpret its central tenets dynamically but truthfully. I offer what follows as an earnest effort to open some paths that will allow faith to assist the moral arc of the universe to bend further towards justice.

---

1. Sanders states, "Midrash was the mode whereby in biblical and later antiquity one explained the world by received tradition properly brought to bear on the situation for which wisdom was sought. It was the world or one's condition which needed illumination, clarification, and explanation, and that was what canonical tradition was for, to make sense of what was going on" (*Canon and Community*, 26). Boyarin claims, "In midrash, emotional and axiological content is released in the process of generating new strings of language out of old beads" (*Intertextuality*, 108).

2. The distinction I make between truth claim and truth value is inspired by, but not precisely the same as, that of Meir Sternberg regarding the two. There he characterizes mixing the two as "loose thinking" (*Poetics of Biblical Narrative*, 300). But while he seems to relate truth value with historicity or the reliability of the history-telling narrative (82), I push the issue of value further to relate to those realities upon which one can stake one's life.

CHAPTER 2

The Origin Stories of Jesus of Nazareth

An effort to clarify what the four Gospels say about Jesus and what they don't affirm.

THE CHRIST STORY ITSELF arises out of an immemorial sense that life itself manifests the *mirabilia dei*—the "wonders of God" and nature that exceed human capacity and comprehension. Today we grasp the length, depth, and breadth of cosmic, physical, and biological evolution with a very different consciousness from our ancestors. But in some ways our knowledge of deep time and deep space does not simply conflict with this ancient perception; rather, it deepens it. For science has uncovered how much the universe is fully relational, not merely inert matter. Its wonders continue to astound even the most astute scientists. Yet too many preachers and teachers still bind themselves to a literalism foreign to the first millennium of how Christians understood revelation. They see themselves engaging in spiritual warfare against these "secular" scientific discoveries. Sadly, they "know not what they do" and should be forgiven. So our task here will delve into how the narratives of Jesus' birth can engage us in wonders that are "ever ancient, ever new."

For the story begins long before the events of 4 BCE and points us in a direction that promises liberation from making false choices as believers. But we need to get there by engaging in some textual sleuthing. Because most people know some version or other of the narrative of Jesus' birth, assumptions abound about its meaning. Some never get beyond a sentimental attachment to memories of earlier Christmas celebrations or the canard "Christmas is for children."

But what if it's not? What if, encoded in these stories, we discover some very adult truths even though they are couched naïvely? This chapter will seek to disassemble the pieces of the story in ways that reveal the various lenses through which Jesus is portrayed. Paying attention to how different texts picture his lineage will alert us about why and how symbols and metaphors carry meanings that delight us and inform our moral imaginations. Here, in our affective minds, the story takes root and begins to grow into a faith commitment.

In fact, the whole arc of the story is already present in Genesis 1's breathtaking poem about the world's creation and its goodness. Despite its early chronological position in the whole Bible, it does not relate a once-for-all event. Genesis, as well as the books later collected as *ta biblia* (in their different forms), never cease to tell a tale of re-creation. The work of God, the Creator, is a constant redo, not an over-and-done effort but the start of reworkings, renewals, and surprises. If this ongoing creative process becomes a closed system of "promise" and "fulfillment" or predestined endings, it slips into banality, convenient for catechetics, but devoid of a deeper grasp of any real truth value, either earlier or now.

So, also, with the words of the prophets, the "classical" figures of the Hebrew *Tanak* or Old Testament Scriptures. Only a comparative anthropologist could adequately uncover the roots of prophecy in soothsaying, divinization, the cultic or law-giving practices behind a Moses, a Samuel, a Nathan, an Elijah, and the like. But as legendary figures whose oracular utterances challenged kings, survived disasters, generated unlikely, even salvific, outcomes, they too take up and reshape the wondrous narrative of death and re-creation. Without the prophetic witness, no Jesus of

Nazareth, no Paul of Tarsus, no Peter the apostle either—in history or in Scripture.

And neither would we have the story of Miriam/Mary or her betrothed, the visionary Joseph, the dream-catcher. Like the dreamer patriarch before him, this latter-day Joseph sees what others cannot and takes a pregnant woman to be his wife. Here, too, we encounter the Gospels' propensity to surround the Jesus story with that sense of wonder that sustained Israel of old and has continued to do so in both the synagogue and the church. Without these stories, the world can readily shrink into a drab place of life-unto-death, an arid desert of impossibilities and dead ends.

But more needs to be said about this sense of the wondrous, or the miraculous, particularly as it surrounds the birth of Jesus. That Jesus was born of a virgin and in Bethlehem are not commensurate details and cannot be reduced to a simple "fact or fiction" binary. Both of these narrative details tell us something about the stories' truth value in their symbolic shape rather than in any literal sense. As above, I use the word "symbolic" here as a technical term. It does not mean "not real" (as the phrase "only symbolic" often asserts). Symbols, like metaphors, expand on the literal meaning of persons or events. They *say* something about the real by associating a thing, event, or person within a wider narrative or a deeper, implicit meaning. Here's an example: Jeremiah the prophet is imprisoned for preaching about Jerusalem's coming destruction by the Babylonians. With conquest imminent, the real estate market has crashed.

Hoping to cash out before it is too late, a relative offers him a piece of the patrimonial property. The prophet accepts and goes through all the trappings of a real estate deal. But, knowing he won't live to enjoy it, he entrusts the deed to his follower Baruch. The gift of the deed symbolizes that the land will be inhabited when the people of Judah return from exile. The literal event is a land transfer; its meaning exceeds the transaction and points beyond itself to a time of redemption and return.

Equivalently, John the Baptist makes his appearance in the desert of Judah dressed in "camel's hair with a leather belt around his waist." Anyone in his day who knew the story of Israel's kings would recognize that the costume revealed him to be the wonder-working prophet Elijah. As seen beforehand by the prophet Malachi, Elijah's reappearance presaged the coming of the day of the Lord, an event of judgment and vindication. John wasn't making a fashion statement. He dressed up and lived as Elijah the prophet had as a sign of an impending crisis, a message that Jesus of Nazareth would take up, yet radically alter.

So when we turn to evaluating the symbol of a virgin birth happening in Bethlehem, we have to face some uncomfortable, but ultimately liberating, literary and theological issues. First, neither Mark nor John (understood to be the first and the final of the canonical Gospels) relate anything about either a miraculous birth or its occurring in the city of David. The author of the Fourth Gospel knew of the tradition that the Messiah should come from Bethlehem, but declared it irrelevant. Birth in this Gospel is always and only "from above," not a geographic or gynecological datum.

Even earlier, Paul the apostle, writing before any of the evangelists, speaks of Jesus only as "descended of the house of David according to the flesh" who was Son of God "born of a woman, born under the law." As far as Jesus' early biography goes in Paul's epistles, that's it. So some of the earliest Christians had no need of either detail to make sense of and to believe in Jesus, "the Word made flesh" who "dwelt among us," who was "made Son of God" by his resurrection. Literal details of his birth are both lacking and unnecessary. And even though Matthew and Luke place Jesus' birth in Bethlehem, their storytelling aims differ significantly.

Matthew's nativity story begins with an angel visiting Joseph in Bethlehem. But it ends in Nazareth in Galilee, where the family has resettled to escape any continuing threat to the child from a jealous Herod. By contrast, Luke starts the story with the angel visiting Mary in Nazareth before a census takes the expectant couple inopportunely to the city of David. After the childbirth and circumcision in Jerusalem, eight days later, they return to Nazareth. In their different ways, both Gospel writers attest to the uncontested fact that Jesus was a Nazorean from Galilee. As does the Fourth Gospel's ironic "Can anything good come out of Nazareth?" But, for these Gospels, the birth in Bethlehem, the city of David, functions as an important symbol of Jesus' messianic identity. It is not, nor does it need to be, a biographical detail to which a historian would or could readily attest. They provide wonderfully artful, but differing, stories whose truth claims as history are weak. Their truth value lies elsewhere.

How, then, can the Christmas narratives and their clearly symbolic portrayal of Jesus' conception and birth make any credible claim for a believer today? For an adequate response, we must briefly engage in some interpretive theory. The stories emerge from a long tradition of authorship where older, authoritative texts served as a prism through which to "see" later events.

In antiquity generally, the past had authority; if writers wanted credibility, they constructed what we now call an *intertext*. New texts interwove, adapted, and reframed older ones in order to authenticate their new/old message. Extensive writings such as the extrabiblical Book of Jubilees and the Testament of Moses both provide vivid examples of how religious authors grappled with unfolding historical crises and hopes, reimagining the past as illuminating the present.

Why are these observations needed to make my point about the symbolic, not literal, value of the nativity narratives? Firstly, because the older texts behind many New Testament affirmations do not themselves relate literal, historical events. Rather they mix earlier legendary and mythic scenarios together in an effort to make sense of the crises or hopes of the writers' own experience. Abraham on Mt. Moriah, Moses before Pharaoh and on Mt. Horeb, or manna in the wilderness, for example, all function, not as history, but as moral, religious, or political tropes. They were written to summon hope, warn of disaster, comfort people in distress, and so on. As symbolic events, they stand in for persons or events whose actual shape remains unrecoverable. They mediate between fact and fiction, but are reducible to neither. Call them "aspirational truths," if you will, but the texts, as texts, relate representational events from a former time. They tell us how earlier writers made sense of life and death struggles, of purpose in the face of chaos, of meanings beyond their easy comprehension.

So Matthew and Luke as narrators built upon a literature replete with unlikely human events that fit into a forward-moving drama of light overcoming darkness, of faith replacing despair. They sought to open their audiences' minds to new imaginative possibilities revealed in "the events that happened among us" (Luke 1:1) by retelling the *mirabilia dei* in a new vein. But they did so before what we call historiography, or a concern for facticity, had been invented. These are modern concepts unavailable to ancient authors for whom even "history" writing included hearsay, admonitions, and morality tales. Even today, writers struggle to capture past events in an evenhanded, credible fashion, devoid of ideology. And often they fail or even ignore such standards.

Both of these evangelists, writing for congregations at least a generation removed from both the Jesus event and from Paul's writings, sought to flesh out the narrative picture and the significance of this unique rabbi from Nazareth. As mentioned previously, the two Gospel accounts have distinct birth and infancy narratives because they were written for different audiences. Matthew, writing for what is called a Jewish-Christian community, modeled Jesus' Davidic lineage on legendary genealogies such as one finds in Genesis. (His own title is *"Biblos Geneseōs"* or "Generational record of Jesus Christ, son of David, son of Abraham.") By contrast, Luke wrote for people of the Roman Empire in its Greco-Roman fullness. As a result, Luke traced Jesus' origins further back to Adam, the first human. Their different purposes account for many of the narrative deviations that influence, but do not compromise, their claims to reveal Jesus' saving identity for the early church. I wish to look briefly at their different storytelling methods before assessing how their truth value survives their mythically framed truth claims.

In Matthew, Mary's pregnancy is revealed to Joseph as a virgin birth based on an earlier, Jewish reinterpretation of an oracle of Isaiah that "a young woman will conceive . . ." (7:14). The original assured King Ahaz that, before a young pregnant woman bore her child (i.e., less than nine months), his enemies would disappear. But in the Alexandrian Jewish version of the Hebrew Isaiah (second-century-BCE Septuagint), this promise was kicked upstairs, as it were. There the "young woman" becomes a "virgin." Why? Because one way that an exiled community of Jews, living among hostile Greek-speakers, upheld their faith was to emphasize the *wondrous*, even miraculous, nature of God's work for his chosen people. In Hellenistic Alexandria virgin births were a common feature in Greco-Roman religious texts, just as they have been in other religious traditions (see the birth of the Buddha). Greek had long been a *lingua franca*, or common vernacular, around the Mediterranean, giving the Greek Bible at least equal status with the original among both Greek-speaking Jews and Gentile religious seekers.

So Matthew inherited a miracle tradition when he cited Isaiah's promise of the virgin birth of Emmanuel (*God-with-us*) as evidence for this new wonder. He used this text despite it literally disagreeing with the angel's instructing Joseph to name the child Jesus (Joshua in Hebrew, meaning "a savior"). He risked the ambiguity because the prophet's oracle illuminated a major theme of his Gospel: "I *am with you* always, even to the end of the age" (28:20). How better to ground Jesus' wondrous presence to his community than in a truly wondrous birth? Over and over, this evangelist cites various prophetic books to fill out the life and work of Jesus. He unfolds his Gospel as a complex intertext, weaving the work and teaching of Jesus out of several sources, but embedding it within an ongoing tradition of revealing the wonders of God, now to be preached to "all nations" (28:19).

Luke's interpretive efforts differ from Matthew as much as his audience does. He does not cite the same Isaiah text. Instead, Luke takes advantage of his Gentile audience's recognizing the phrase "good news" (*euangelia*) as the birth announcement of a royal heir. Here the betrothed virgin is to give birth to the Davidic Messiah. Mary's "How can this be?" provokes the angel Gabriel's answer that echoes an even earlier dialogue. In Genesis, when a doubting Sarah questions her unlikely pregnancy, the messenger asks her (rhetorically): "Is anything too marvelous for the Lord to do?" (18:14). So Luke's latter-day messenger answers Mary's own question with the affirmative response that "nothing is impossible with God." The echo of the earlier wonder is unmistakable and draws out Mary's surrender to her service (1:37–8). But once the angel leaves, Mary quickly looks for her own two-factor authentication by rushing to check out the angel's news about another unlikely pregnancy: that of elderly Elizabeth (herself a Sarah-like figure). For if Elizabeth is pregnant, so is Mary! Luke then pens Mary's response, both to her cousin's condition and to her own, by reprising the prophet Samuel's mother's hymn of praise (now Mary's *Magnificat*). Luke's intertextual tales, here and elsewhere, rates him as a first-class screenwriter long before his time.

But it's important to note that we are not talking fairy tales here. Rather, both authors, writing for different audiences, artistically introduce into the story of Jesus of Nazareth mythic events that reveal God's wondrous presence in and among recognizable human beings. The narratives possess truth value despite their being couched in legendary and mythic frameworks. For they ground the wondrous works of God in public and accessible features of reality: in genealogy, chronology, geography, and history-like details.

Luke's portrayal of the Annunciation is said to be the most frequently painted one in all Western art: a heavenly messenger announces a birth without benefit of a human father to which the maiden gives her free assent. It contravenes the entire masculine-dominated tilt of politics and religion, giving agency to a woman in the divine scheme to "cast down the mighty from their thrones and raise the lowly" (1:52). Her song foreshadows Jesus' own message of blessing for the poor and woe for the wealthy (6:20, 24). The mythic elements, while too easily dismissed today, undergird a strong message about a future state of society that is both just and inclusive. Both authors have engaged in storytelling as a form of prophetic challenge that sows seeds for social change, if not for a revolution, in human affairs. The stories continue to have expressive power because they avoid political theory, philosophical argument, or metaphysical definitions. They engage in wonder to prompt their readers to act upon a future history revealed in these timeless, mythic events.

At the same time, neither Matthew nor Luke can be accused of creating the fetish that arose in later centuries for elevating virginity over sexual generation as a privileged condition of sanctity in Christian and human life. Others bear responsibility for that: fanatics such as the second-century North African Tertullian, enthusiasts such as Origen of Alexandria, powerful churchmen like Ambrose of Milan, and Neoplatonic philosophers like St. Augustine. These men all used these stories as a cudgel to promote their crusade against late Hellenistic sexual hedonism as they understood it.

Their flesh vs. spirit view of sex joined with the early monastic ideal of world-denial, itself a social protest against a violent and debased society. Despite the grains of truth in these criticisms, casting human sexuality as encapsulating "the weakness of the flesh" has had long and tragic consequences. But neither Gospel authors should catch the blame for these excesses. Their message outlives its reduction to a biological sleight of hand that devalues human sexuality. Both Mary's courage, and the love that Joseph expressed in taking in a single mother and sheltering her child, should themselves be counted as one of the wondrous events in the story of the origins of Jesus of Nazareth.

Let me summarize my argument thus far for interpreting these elements of the Christmas story symbolically as opposed to reducing them to mere fiction or insisting on them as actual fact. Today, we no longer base our worldview, our grasp of reality itself, on the cosmology, anthropology, or biology that biblical writers took for granted. Only unreconstructed fundamentalist believers understand the physical origins of the universe via a literal reading of Genesis chapter 1 or 2. These early, poetic creation tales continue to have truth value about the created world, and even the human condition, quite separate from their unscientific, counterfactual basis. Their value lies in their poetic, not their literal, meaning. Equivalently, we should not base our understanding of Jesus' birth on a first-century notion of conception, miraculous or otherwise.

This I Believe

To hold, today, that Jesus of Nazareth was not born with two sets of chromosomes from a father and a mother contravenes the far more basic belief in his full humanness. His putative virgin birth represented two of the four evangelists' mode of telling a first-century audience that his life, from unlikely birth to gruesome death and beyond, expresses an unprecedented revelation of divine love. It does not, at base, represent a biological fact. Its power does not reside in Mary's sexless conception of her son, but in the story's world-altering trajectory.

Beyond the faith conviction that all humans bear "the image and likeness of God," the good news avers that this man, born of this Jewish woman, bears that identity as a unique guarantee of the innate sacredness embedded in all living things. As Emmanuel, Savior, Son of God, and Messiah, Jesus is also the son of a single mother, born in poverty, soon a refugee from political persecution. He would grow up to be an itinerant preacher "with nowhere to lay his head." His lowly powerlessness has laid down one of the most formidable challenges to this world's mighty ones who lord it over others. Even as an infant he generates a promise of and challenge to world-reversal that seeks to bring God's justice to bear on the very shape of human society. His story is both prototype and archetype: unique to him and his own, but adaptable in numerous crises, perils, and hope-filled settings, historical, present, and to come.

For her part, the Blessed Virgin Mary—herself a female symbolic figure *par excellence*—has played a unique role in Christian history, art, and theology. Her personal spiritual agency, from the Middle Ages onward, grew precisely because her person explicitly expressed the divine feminine. As God-bearer (*Theotokos* in Greek), she anchored a highly abstracted belief in the nature of divinity within the universal experience of our birth from woman. In her, the sentiment we accord mothers meets a generative power that shares in the very nature of God. But holding these two seeming opposites of virginity and motherhood in tandem has itself spawned an ambiguous tradition of belief and practice when they are literally mismatched. On the one hand, she proclaims the centrality and dignity of the feminine. But, on the other, claiming her virginity was "perpetual" has tended to subvert the vital role and beauty of female sexuality to the detriment of both church and society.

Still, the nativity stories in the two Gospels continue to have value, precisely because of their mythic form. They fill out and balance the Fourth Gospel's affirmation that "the Word was made flesh and dwelled among us" with the story of a woman and a "just" man through whose love divinity became flesh. For no one can be "born again of water and the Spirit" or "reborn from above" before being given the gift of biological and affective life. Mary's role, as necessary as any mother's, has raised her in Christian belief to bear the title, as above (but in Latin) *Mater Dei*. She is the unique human being through whom our essential selves, our souls, our very species enjoy this unique act of divine self-giving.

All subsequent elaborations of the role that Mary of Nazareth plays in the Christian story build upon her uniqueness. But theology has often struggled to keep up with her affective hold on believers whose "sense of the faith" elaborated the feminine character of divine grace. As *Notre Dame*, she has raised basilicas and cathedrals, offers shelter in faith's storms, and appears in visions to comfort the afflicted. Yet too often her emotional appeal has underplayed her Gospel role to afflict the comfortable. As we continue to trace the outlines of the Christian story in the Creed, I am seeking to reweave her story as mother and myth into the full narrative of God's kingdom and its justice.

This issue of faith's mythic language, which I have introduced, will again come sharply into focus as we seek to mine one of the early "symbols of the faith," the Apostles' Creed, for its truth value. With one exception, I will use the simpler version than the fourth-century formula adopted at the Council of Nicaea (and subsequently amended). The Apostles' Creed encompasses the Christ story, but expands that story backward to Genesis and forward to the book of Revelation and beyond. Again, my task will explore the ways in which its essentially mythic and symbolic formulation allows it to remain fresh today and worthy of prayerful adherence.

This I Believe

Like the Gospel narratives themselves, the mythic form it celebrates reaches into the past only to reconfigure believers' future hope and to summon their commitment to faith and effective love, i.e., justice for all creation.

CHAPTER 3

Extending the Narrative
The Apostles' Creed

I present a brief explanation of the Creed's role in fleshing out the Christ story before undertaking a journey through its crucial elements.

NO ONE VERSION OF the Creed can narrate the full spectrum of Christian belief. In fact, the history of the various creeds might itself fill a volume. Still, the version called "the Apostles' Creed" avoids the more philosophically accented affirmations sparked in the fourth and fifth centuries by controversies about Christ's divine identity. Hence, it represents a *precis* or summary of what a believing Christian affirms. As just mentioned, I have replaced the final two affirmations with those contained in the Nicene-Constantinopolitan version (381 AD), which, I believe, retain more closely the biblical language behind them (see note 3 below).

I believe in God,
the Father almighty,
Creator of heaven and earth,

and in Jesus Christ, God's only Son, our LORD,
who was conceived by the Holy Spirit,

This I Believe

born of the Virgin Mary,
suffered under Pontius Pilate,
was crucified, died and was buried;
he descended into hell;
on the third day he rose again from the dead;
he ascended into heaven,
and is seated at the right hand of God the Father almighty;
from there he will come to judge the living and the dead.

I believe in the Holy Spirit,
the holy catholic church,
the communion of saints,
the forgiveness of sins,
I look for the resurrection of the dead,
and the life of the world-to-come.[1]
Amen.

Let me begin with a brief look at the Creed's function in the earliest days of the Christian church. While its text continued to develop into the eighth century, the earliest form seems to have arisen in the context of an examen for catechumens, or candidates for baptism. We have to put ourselves back into those early centuries as local communities began to form, mostly under the radar of imperial pagan cultic practice. While signing on as a Christian did not always and everywhere expose a person to legal jeopardy, it is clear that there was some risk involved in membership in this *religio illicita*, an illegal religion, dubbed a dangerous cult. The Creed told a story whose truth claims anchored a person's affiliation within this marginalized group accused of atheism. Beyond that, one was joining a larger community whose disparate social, ethnic, and economic groups claimed to be "catholic," or universal. Its universality also implied a cosmic communion with the divine.

---

1. The last two phrases are drawn from the longer and perhaps earlier Nicene-Constantinopolitan version. They spell out the hope for *the resurrection of the dead* in place of *the resurrection of the body* and for *the life of the world-to-come* rather than *eternal life*. The reasons for my adopting these phrases will be clearer in the explications that follow.

Extending the Narrative

What benefit would be gained by someone willing to take the risk? First, it seems that standard pagan religious devotion fulfilled a political role more than any genuine, personal, or communitarian one. Experiencing a deeper solidarity with one's fellows had great appeal, as the existence of many so-called mystery cults throughout the empire attests. Next to all these groups, worship of Zeus and friends, never mind the Roman emperor himself, did not create any warm and fuzzy feelings. Pinching incense on a sacrificial fire—the minimum act required by pagan authorities—ignored the individual persons' life circumstances, or their fate in a power- and wealth-crazed society. Legal religion required sacrificial adherence. It did not offer any ultimate coherence with one's own desires, passions, or loves.

So when early communities that professed Christ practiced *diakonia*, the obligation to exercise service to others, their beliefs rearranged social relationships at a profound level. The church, in some of its earliest forms, comprised a mutual aid society. House churches functioned as community centers where all were accepted. Emperor Julian, Constantine's nephew who reverted to the worship of Rome's pantheon of gods, begrudgingly admired how "the Galileans" took care not only of their own sick, but of pagan believers as well! In fact, he complained to his own clergy that they needed to emulate their rivals![2] As has been the case, before and since, other forces and influences have compromised those who make these religious affirmations. But, at base, Christianity rises or falls on its ability to offer truths about creation, life, death, and humanity's place in the cosmos. How this remains true in the twenty-first century is the task I take up in these pages.

---

2. Hart, a scholar of antiquity, credits Julian with "a real and commendable love of Hellenistic civilization, as well as a touching inability to recognize that the religious forms of that civilization were largely exhausted" (*Atheist Delusions*, 186–91).

This I Believe

God: Creator and Triune

The full doctrine of God replaces "Almighty" with "Communion" as the essential New Testament revelation.

*I believe in God,
the Father almighty,
Creator of heaven and earth . . .*

In English, our word "believe" has a different derivation from the noun "faith," which tends to be used more than the noun "belief." As unrelated cognates, the two words lose some of the connotation of the equivalent Greek verb and noun *pisteuô/pistis*. Today, we use the word "believe" to express an opinion (commonly no different from a belief), to offer a surmise, or to think over things, such as who will most likely win the Super Bowl. It might even mean, "I'll bet on it!" in the sense that I'm willing to take the risk I'm wrong. This sense is captured in the popular understanding of "Pascal's wager." Though Blaise Pascal deserves better, his "pensée," or thought experiment, surmised that it was worth leading a moral life because it should lead one to be worthy of an eternal reward. But if there were no such reward in store (i.e., there is no divine judge of moral conduct), then one would have lost nothing as you would have led your life as a good human being.[3]

But the verbal form of "faith" that appears as "I believe" means something more than a mental guess that something is right. It expresses personal trust, a deeper, more internal, and even emotional commitment. It calls forth a person's understanding of where he or she/they see themselves located within the totality of humanity's lived experience. Unlike popular slogans from retailers or sports teams that scream "Believe" without any particular object, religious faith as expressed in the Creed always has a singular object, and a "credible" one at that. Nevertheless, as we will shortly examine more fully, the word "God" pales as a descriptor of the reality that calls forth this faith.

---

3. Pascal, *Pensées*, II, 418.

Extending the Narrative

"I believe" does not profess the intellectual proposition that God, an entity whose existence as another, superior being/person, exists as an object of ideological loyalty. A deeper tradition of theological reflection on the "question" of God refuses to recognize the framing of prayer or belief within the confines of an othering subject/object relationship. Martin Buber's insight into religious faith as a subject-to-subject communion itself updated the earlier mystics' experience of a "hidden wholeness" (Merton) in the fabric of existence: that God is *in* everything and that everything is *in* God.[4] The divine as Being itself (Aquinas) or the Ground of Being (Tillich) does not admit of a cosmic or metaphysical disjunction between us creatures (and all of the created universe) from the Source of all that is. Here, "I believe" invokes one's own acceptance of an invitation to live in communion with reality at its most integral level. An ideological commitment to particular religious tenets lies outside the scope of this first of the Creed's affirmations.

When the ancient formula used the additional epithet, "the Father... Creator of heaven and earth," it was adapting the worldview of the book of Genesis, where heaven and earth arose from an act of divine self-expression. But neither the title "Father" nor the ascription "Almighty" appear in Genesis 1. Their being teamed up occurred gradually. Divine paternity emerged early when Samuel the prophet declared King David the Lord's (adopted) son (2 Sam 7:14). "Son" (of God) then became a royal title as witnessed in the enthronement song "You are my son; this day I have begotten you" (Ps 2:7). In time, Israel, the people, were said to have been the "son" called from Egypt (Hos 11:1). This communal adoption is explicit in Malachi 2:10: "Have we not all one father? Has not one God created us?"

In the period between the prophets and the New Testament writings, it became more common to ascribe fatherhood to God, both individually of the persecuted just one (Wis 2:16) and in a

---

4. Borg defines this position as *panentheism*, which distinguishes itself from *pantheism* or the conviction that everything is God. "But pan*en*theism affirms both transcendence (God otherness or moreness) and immanence (God's presence).... God is all around us and within us, and we are within God" (*God We Never Knew*, 32).

sailor's prayer recounting God's providence in the same book (14:3). Jesus calling upon God as his "dear Father" (*'abba*) led, then, directly to the early community's glorifying "the God and Father of our Lord Jesus Christ" (Rom 15:6) and their belief in their own adoption enacted in their crying out "Abba! Father!" (Rom 8:15).

Fewer names or terms have a more obvious metaphorical significance than "father," but that has not prevented a host of patriarchal, and blatantly sexist, denotations to be attached to it. Again, the problem is with its literalness and how this allowed it to become an oppressive arm of male-only, paternalist structures in church and society. Of course, long before "father" attached itself to Zeus and his fractious family, a shift had occurred from depth being numinous to height: from Earth Mother to Sky Father as some have speculated. When cities arose and the power of headmen or kings asserted themselves, religion began a journey that has tipped along the way into idolatry. Monotheism and monolatry, the worship of the one with power over others, can collapse into each other, especially when words, art, and religious reasoning loose themselves from their metaphorical moorings.[5]

The metaphor of Father, as it become part of the Creed, expresses relationality between the Creator and creation, between what the Latin term *Genitor* ("Begetter") captures and the one who comes forth, hence Son ("Begotten"). Over the centuries, Christian theology has tended to force these metaphors into some ontological scheme or other. Perhaps because, in our time, fatherhood has revealed its seamier and even dangerous manifestations, even the metaphor has become tainted. The feminist critique has been a necessary counterweight, then, to too much literalness, too insidious a desire to project images of greatness onto intimations of transcendence.

But, even when we maintain this well-worn paternal metaphor, we need not do the same with "Almighty" because the story

---

5. Armstrong affirms that because its chief symbol of the divine is a personalized deity, "Idolatry has always been one of the pitfalls of monotheism" (*Case for God*, 321).

behind it differs significantly. Rather, this adjective was derived from *El Shaddai*, seeming to name the "God of the Mountains," perhaps originally a Canaanite nature god. Used as another name for the Hebrew *YHWH* ("I Am Who I Am") revealed to Moses (Exod 3:14), the designation became inflated to the cosmological and quasi-metaphysical *pantokrator* when rendered Greek, later yielding the familiar Latin *omnipotens*, both signifying "all-powerful." But this epithet (in English) "Almighty" rarely appears in the New Testament, and never in the mouth of Jesus or the writings of Paul. The book of Revelation uses it when citing the Greek version of a Hebrew psalm or in its very Hebraic liturgical hymns. Rather "God" appears as "Abba/Father" in the Gospels and epistles without the ascription "Almighty" as captured in the Creed.

In other words, "God" as a generic term for a divine being often means someone very different from the One whom Jesus of Nazareth addressed as "dear Father." What's more, though "God" is used to translate one of the names of the Creator in the Hebrew Scriptures, it remains a generic term, not a name at all. The divine name remains unpronounced out of reverence, with "Lord" or "The Holy One, Blessed Be He" spoken in its place. Even today, observant Jews write "G-d" rather than traverse proper reverence. What I'm getting at is that, along with various Hebrew ascriptions, Christianity also inherited a generic, pagan notion of God, the Almighty. Over time, the intimate and unspoken YHWH (a bridegroom and lover in the prophets) and the caritive *Abba* in the New Testament gave way before notions of divine power and might.

When Roman forms of prayer, in particular, became addressed to "Almighty, Eternal, God," they distanced the pray-er from the Prayee. This orientation introduced what I have termed a form of "othering" that objectifies God, opening a cosmic gap between the deity and those supplicating the divine. "God" loses its metaphorical force and pretends to name a literal numinous reality, a Supreme Being. "A being greater than which no being can exist" framed the "ontological argument" of the medieval Anselm of Canterbury, who offered it as a so-called proof of God's existence. Thus did a revealed source of life and love become an interesting conundrum in the service of the new fashion for rational philosophy.[6]

This problem of "God" language became real for me as I peered out from the dome of Michelangelo's imposing papal mausoleum we know as St. Peter's in the Vatican. Looking down from the lantern of the dome, I noticed the inscription "DOM" on some roof tiles. When I inquired, I discovered that the acronym arose in the days of the pre-Christian Roman Republic, saluting *Deus Optimus Maximus*, "the Greatest and Highest God," i.e., Jupiter (Zeus in Greek). As far as I know, Jupiter is credited with having many children, but he never claimed paternity in the case of Jesus of Nazareth! Gazing out over the Eternal City from that height, I found myself contemplating the even higher irony involved in this miscast tribute to a pagan deity.

But, let's face it, beginning the Creed with a profession of God's omnipotence or almightiness has caused havoc for religious believers for the past few centuries. As "Almighty," God has become the focus of the problem known as "theodicy," i.e., how do we justify the notion of an omnipotent/good God with the fact of evil in the world? We might choose to chase this problem down a philosophical rabbit hole, but we need not do so. History and science have come to our rescue or, at least, have introduced a note of enlightened humility into our efforts to square this circle. Galileo's discoveries and Isaac Newton's laws describing nature's physically determinate properties retired God's role as a causal, universal Arbiter or Fixer. Previously, pregnancy meant that God "opened the womb"; storms, droughts, locust plagues, etc. flowed from God's angry nostrils; kings, armies, victories and defeats—all bowed before or were caused by an inescapable divine will.

Understood literally, natural causality would make the God of the Bible a monster, drunk on his own power and attached to his own willfulness. Early in the modern era, deists such as Thomas Jefferson and Thomas Paine used a fallback position that preserved

---

6. Armstrong describes Anselm of Laon (later Archbishop of Canterbury) in this way; "Excited by the new vogue for reasoning, he wanted to make traditional Christian teaching rationally coherent." See her explanation of his "ontological proof" for God's existence (*Case for God*, 131–32).

a noninvolved clockmaker Creator in God's role. But then atheists famously claimed that the hypothesis that any such existed was no longer needed and society would now emerge more pacifically.[7] "Things happen" either through the random collision of atoms or via predetermined actions or responses that eliminated any conscious agency at all, divine or human. Reason may have been enthroned on the altar of Notre Dame during the French Revolution, but Random Fate came to reign supreme in the twentieth century.[8]

To my mind, the biggest break in this dilemma of cause and effect occurred with the discovery of, and reflection upon, the principle of development or natural evolution. At first, most Christian believers reacted with horror at the notion—clearly some people we call fundamentalists still do. But wiser thinkers, such as the nineteenth-century thinker John Henry Newman, understood *development* to be at the heart of how the divine manifests itself in the world.[9] Life itself means change, he wrote fourteen years before Darwin published *The Origin of Species*. Direct divine causality does not lie behind natural or historical events. Even medieval theologian Thomas Aquinas distinguished primary causality (God's ultimate creative action) from secondary causalities that had specific effects in the natural and human world. Thomas and the realistic philosophical school that he represents hold that the natural world has its own intelligibility: while natural elements

---

7. Taylor quotes from the eighteenth-century writer de La Metrie's *L'Homme Machine* and his argument for atheism as sounding the death knell of "Providential Deism" (*Secular Age*, 293).

8. Goldblatt credits the Renaissance's rediscovery of Lucretius's *On the Nature of Things* as reintroducing atomism, how "atoms moving randomly through space" explain how and why things are (*Swerve*, 5 and throughout). Mlodinow sums up his impressive study of probability theory and the basic concepts of randomness "to illustrate how they apply to human affairs" and "the ubiquitous role of random processes in our lives" (*Drunkard's Walk*, 217). Everything may not be the result of fate, but appreciating both good luck and "the random events that contribute to our success" (219) can help us negotiate life's random contingencies.

9. Ker quoting his 1845 *Essay on the Development of Christian Doctrine*: "In a higher world it is otherwise, but here below to live is to change, and to be perfect is to have changed often" (*Newman*, 304).

exhibit constancy and stability, life also unfolds through contingent and unstable events and developments. Likewise, historical events occur dependent on both circumstances and human choices. They do not unfold as predetermined by God's fixed will, nor by Hegel's spiritual nor Marx's materialist dialectic.

Therefore, accepting the cosmos as it is requires that believers account for randomness as well as order in any adequate theology of creation. For the natural order is composed of both order and chaos, Newtonian physics and subatomic randomness, predictability and quantum indeterminacy. Without these balancing forces, the freedom of the natural world to be itself, and the moral freedom that self-conscious human beings exhibit, would be compromised. The resulting life-world would live under the thrall of a dreadful mechanical doom.

No God worthy of recognition or worship could be responsible for the political and social life-world where a long list of evil -isms manifest themselves over and over again. Is this "the best of all possible worlds," as Leibniz claimed and Voltaire mocked? My guess is that the story is still unfolding and is best answered humbly yet hopefully. We no longer aspire to the conquest of the natural world or to the elimination of all evils. But we can assume some responsibility for upholding the inherent plurality of goodness that has lived, from the beginning, in both the natural and moral realms that we call "creation." In the One God, there is a diversity of mutual acceptance and love, a love, as Dante describes in his final Vision "which moves the sun and the other stars" (the last line of his *Paradiso*).[10]

But we also know that creation far outstrips either Dante's poetic language or the "heaven and earth" of the Bible's worldview: one Sun, not the billions that have been discovered in the vastness of the physical cosmos. At the same time, this difference, as vast as it seems, need not affect what our faith affirms. For while Genesis tended to limit creation to the visible realm, it presumed a world beyond, and the later Nicene version of the Creed expanded what God created to encompass "all things visible and invisible."

---

10. Dante Alighieri, *Divine Comedy* 3, 347.

Extending the Narrative

Clearly, those fifth-century thinkers hardly conceived of quarks, neutrinos, dark energy, or galaxies beyond counting. But all these forces, including dark matter and black holes, fit the Creed's inclusive vision. We can even say that should we discover life and intelligence on other worlds, it would not inherently challenge the expansiveness of the doctrine of creation contained in this first, simple formula of the ancient Apostles' Creed.

This is true because, at heart, the doctrine of creation, so called, does not name a *past* event dated to either thirteen billion or six thousand some odd years ago. That God "rested" after six days of fashioning the world served several functions in the ancient world. It argued against other myths of creation that depended on murder or on physical/sexual conflict. But it also established the practice of the Sabbath, a day of rest that received divine approbation in the opening chapter of the Bible. The weekend would not come for centuries, but the text gave Hebrew society a basis for ruling out a seven-day workweek!

Other voices and traditions in the Bible never accepted this fixed notion of the heavens and the earth and all their array as anything but the start of a process whose fulfillment lay in the future. Some texts of promise focused on the vindication or salvation of an oppressed people and a refounded nation. Others reimagined things on a much more cosmic scale, envisioning divine action that would bring about "new heavens and a new earth," a redeemed world both continuous with, but also radically different from, the first creation.

Though we today are convinced of the future orientation of human consciousness, the doctrine of creation beat us to it. Creation presumes an unfolding or an evolution of an open-ended process of the universe's coming to know itself.[11] We know that this

---

11. Haught states, "Furthermore, there is no reason to insist that evolution has come anywhere near the end of its journey. If you look under your feet, behind your back, and over your head, you will see a new type of organizational complexity now taking shape. Teilhard calls this latest evolutionary level of being the 'noosphere'... Perhaps, for all we know, evolutionary creation is still at the cosmic dawn" ("Teilhard, Cosmic Purpose, and the Search for Extraterrestrial Intelligence," 15).

This I Believe

realization far outstrips our capacities for description. But futurists of all sorts continue to predict a looming state of world affairs when technology will merge with and/or overwhelm human society. While most such ideas depend on a materialist understanding of the universe, they seem to agree that Aristotle's "arrow of time" moves toward some un-understood goal. Belief in the "Creator of heaven and earth" remains open to such an Unknown, particularly if we take into account the ultimate shape of the Creed's notion of God.

Writing more than fifty years ago, the Jesuit theologian Karl Rahner advocated banning the use of the word "God" for fifty years. But we need to give his protest at least another fifty years because we consistently shrink the mystery of divine Communion, as a mutual sharing in life-giving love, when we reduce it to the generic title "God." Nor is it always enough for Christians to expand on this shrunken notion of deity by invoking the "Trinity" or the "Triune God." While both these terms have profound implications for naming how we share in the gift of divinity, they often reduce an expression about the deepest Mystery to a mathematical conundrum. Puzzling over either of these terms disguises, rather than reveals, our own *communio* or sharing in the divine nature of all that is real. As we examine the tripartite shape of the Creed, we will see how this mystery of shared love deepens any adequate notion of the God as revealed in Christ and by the Spirit.

One more note about how Christianity conceives of God's nature or being as it was formulated in the conciliar debates (and politics) that roiled the early church: The word "person" came to be used to describe a distinction in the one God between the Father/Creator, Word/Son/Redeemer, and Paraclete/Spirit. But this antique use of "person" leads to a misunderstanding of the One in whom, as well as, to whom we pray. To us, the word "person" indicates a unique individual with a "personality" and "free will" (more or less). But, as I understand it, the three-person-in-one-God formula was adopted specifically to capture a paradox: to maintain the monotheism of the earlier revelation (*Adonai echad*, "the Lord alone" in Deuteronomy 6:4) but to deny the plurality of pagan gods. At the same time, a form of Eastern theology sought to capture the dynamic quality in the Godhead by using the metaphor of individual but mutual *energies*, through which the natural and human world experience how divinity manifests itself. As a less static metaphor, the concept can help expand our simplistic acceptance of divine "personhood."[12]

"Three-persons-in-one-God" represents a hyper-philosophical solution to naming the mystery of the divine communion at the heart of Transcendence. It lacks the intimacy embedded in Paul's "the grace of our Lord Jesus Christ, the love of God, and the communion of the Holy Spirit" (2 Cor 13:13) now poured out upon humanity. Yet it attempts to profess the integrity of created reality in God's Oneness, while also expressing the relationality in the One that spills over into the universe of all things.

We know today that all the energy in the universe exists in the relationship between its component parts, that life emerges through a feedback loop in the life of cells. So the Source of all that is must also be relational at heart: a Trinity of Infinity, Imminence, and Intimacy as the theologian Richard Rohr casts it. In God, we discover neither monism which subsumes all reality, nor a binary dualism that presumes conflict, but a relational Threeness that reveals "an intrinsic plurality to goodness."[13] This same author cites the poly-scientist J. B. S. Haldane in a provocative analogy to what has been termed the "mystery" of the Trinity: "Now, my own suspicion is that the universe is not only queerer than we suppose, but queerer than we can suppose."[14]

In this "queer" universe, all created things remain free to be themselves—at least this is the way I read the realist tradition in philosophy and theology. But this freedom is perfected in

---

12. Weil has a startling take on the inadequacy of the term when she writes, "One is able to think of God at the same time, not successively, as being three and one . . . only by thinking of Him at the same time as personal and impersonal . . . Saints of very lofty spirituality, like St. John of the Cross, have seized simultaneously and with equal force both the personal and impersonal aspects of God" (*Letter,* 20).

13. Rohr, *Divine Dance,* 61.

14. Quoted from Haldane, "Possible Worlds," in Rohr, *Divine Dance,* 72.

understanding the relational character of all that is. The Trinity underlies the Christian understanding of what Buddhism calls *inter-being*, our basic relatedness with all created and living things. To believe in the God revealed as Trinity is to commit to an inner mutuality of the divine and human, to refuse mastery, and to see our "power" as vulnerability. Such is the paradox Paul cited in 1 Corinthians: God's weakness or vulnerability-in-relationship has more potential energy than any human wisdom or power to be life-giving (1:25).

Conceived by the Holy Spirit, Born of the Virgin Mary

> *and in Jesus Christ, God's only Son, our* LORD,
> *who was conceived by the Holy Spirit,*
> *born of the Virgin Mary,*

> *Mary's symbolic role grows when the physical miracle of virgin birth takes a back seat.*

The second section of the Creed contains the full scope of the Christ story, which begins here with his so-called virginal conception. In this section, the phrases "suffered under Pontius Pilate, was crucified, died and was buried" can claim historical veracity and so lie outside my current efforts. At present, efforts to affirm that these statements weave an elaborate fiction do not garner much support.[15] An abundance of corroborating evidence predicts that any herald of the dawning reign of God, such as John the Baptist, Qumran's Teacher of Righteousness, or Simon bar Kokhba in the next century, would meet a similar fate. But beyond Jesus of Nazareth's execution, we must turn to the language of myth, symbol, and metaphor to grasp what believers are affirming. Without these linguistic tools, the story of Jesus of Nazareth gets whittled down

---

15. Wright, in his extensive summary of various "quests" for the historical Jesus, affirms that presently, "Jesus must be understood as a comprehensible and yet, so to speak, crucifiable first-century Jew, whatever the theological or hermeneutical consequences" (*Jesus*, 86).

Extending the Narrative

to the philosophe's version that Thomas Jefferson, the devout deist, created. He literally cut up two volumes of the New Testament, cutting and pasting the "philosophical" passages and excising any of the texts' miraculous content. In deism's perspective, "Christ" becomes a surname, nothing more.

Many scholars of language and religion have argued more persuasively that I did in an earlier work *Beyond Naïve Belief* that we cannot communicate as intelligent beings without these ways of crafting meaning for our lives.[16] Human experience cannot be adequately articulated by what Karen Armstrong, the internationally known religious scholar, defines as "the pragmatic mode of thought that enabled people to function effectively in the world."[17] As crucial as practical logic/scientific understanding remains for surviving and thriving as individuals and societies, a second mode—that of *mythos*—fills out our intellectual and affective repertoire.

But I would press the case further. Biblical faith's real subject matter presents itself mainly in texts that themselves refer to other texts or renditions of religious experience. As such, biblical texts not only employ but themselves function as *metaphors*, pointing beyond themselves for their full coherence. They always suffer from a necessary distinction between reality itself and our ability to grasp and convey the full scope of the real. In fact, metaphors, by definition, are literally false as a condition of their conveying any truth value whatsoever.[18] They witness to a necessary asymmetry between words and things/reality, even in so far as it is knowable. Especially when faith traditions attempt to speak about what is ultimate, the divine, or even the deepest truths about the human

16. Dinter, *Beyond Naïve Belief*, 27–28.
17. Armstrong, *Case for God*, xi.
18. Dinter citing Paul Ricoeur's theory of the "whispered no" in metaphor and symbol: "Though symbols violate the logic of the law of the excluded middle by which something cannot be true and not true at the same time, they are not any more of a mystery than the principle of indeterminacy which violates the laws of classical physics" (*Beyond Naïve Belief*, 209). Kimmerer quotes scientist and poet Jeffrey Burton Russell, "as a sign of a deeper truth, metaphor was close to sacrament. Because the vastness and richness of reality cannot be expressed by the overt sense of a statement alone" (*Braiding Sweetgrass*, 46).

condition, they always confront a boundary or limitation. For instance, "the human spirit" or "the soul," though time-honored metaphors, cannot adequately describe, but can only refer to, some plus-factor in the common human experience of the self.

But, for its part, scientific discourse also enjoys a persistent gap between its current ideas or hypotheses and objective reality *in toto*. In fact, scientific inquiry depends on this asymmetry to guarantee the open-ended nature of its efforts. For science cannot demonstrate the full validity of its theories of the universe from within the universe itself. As a result of these inherent limitations, for all its significant discoveries about life's physical mysteries, scientific research in itself cannot provide objective answers to the questions of life and death that provoke the persistence of mythos, poetry, and art itself in human religion and culture.

I am contending that this open-endedness represents a correlative boundary with the unfolding nature of religious truth. In both instances, the gap between our *ideas* and the reality they seek to grasp (transcendent or otherwise) actually mirror each other. In their different, but not adversative ways, religion and science are both provisional discourses, requiring patience for a fuller or deeper understanding of the desired objects of their quests.[19]

Believers might actually be made more uncomfortable with these limitations than scientists are. Theological statements seek to do an end run around this boundary, but these efforts too often reflect something that C. S. Lewis once observed about prayer when he wrote:

> All prayers always, taken at their word, blaspheme . . .
> And all are idolators, crying unheard
> To senseless idols, if thou take them at thy word . . .
> Take not, O Lord, our literal sense. Lord, in thy great
> Unspoken speech our limping metaphor translate.[20]

---

19. Haught affirms, "The cosmos is a book still being written, and so we *cannot* yet read it with full comprehension, either through the eyes of science or through those of theology. Both disciplines are humbled by the vast distances the universe apparently has ahead of it" (*Deeper Than Darwin*, 53).

20. Lewis, *Pilgrim's Regress*, 145.

Extending the Narrative

For taken "at their word," all our literal readings, either of materialist scientific data or of ancient religious texts, fall flat. Instead let us exult in our imperfect metaphors that save us from all manner of reductionism. In fact, they can fully complement practical logic/scientific analyses meant to help humans survive and thrive in perilous times.[21]

For example, the science of climate change, for all its predictive power, has rarely changed people's minds about how they live day-to-day. Mythic or metaphorical narratives may help in this task when stats, charts, and scientific papers do not draw enough attention to motivate a reluctant body politic. To claim that the Earth itself, our Mother, has been grievously wounded can move people in an affective way to make real changes in their life decisions. Our emotional attachment to the biome, to plants, forests, birds, wild animals, clean air, and water generate the stories that can convert consumers into caregivers.[22]

In the same vein, art and music, central to both aesthetic and religious expression, all exceed the limitations of scientific reason and the appeal of human rationality. In some forms, they reveal the limitations of language itself, putting us in touch with the ineffable, something we can feel but never fully know. Without symbolic language and imagery, we remain earthbound and far less motivated to enlarge our thought-world and to engage in meaningful, moral action.

When we look at the Creed's further affirmations about Jesus after his death on the cross, we are squarely in the realm of the mythic. That he was "conceived of the holy Spirit, born of the Virgin Mary . . . descended into hell, rose from the dead, ascended

---

21. Edelman, a neuroscientist, speaks of "two main modes of thought—logic and selectionism (or pattern recognition)," the latter of which lies behind our metaphorical abilities. He sees a "balance between these two modes of thought" as the basis for consciousness, which he terms "our greatest gift" (*Wider Than the Sky*, 147–8).

22. Kimmerer proposes, "The earth, that first among good mothers, gives us the gift that we cannot provide ourselves . . . She gives what we need without being asked. I wonder if she gets tired, old Mother Earth. Or if she too is fed by the giving" (*Braiding Sweetgrass*, 103).

into heaven, and is seated at the right hand of God and will come to judge the living and the dead" all occur outside the realm of natural or historical truth claims. As such, we cannot limit ourselves to *logical* or purely historical factuality to grasp their actual truth value. We look, instead, at these events symbolically to understand what they say about the life and identity of Jesus beyond his historical life and death in ancient Palestine/Israel. If we were to limit the meaning and impact of these affirmations to the physically possible, we would deprive believers of any transcendent basis of their own identities as well as many of their personal, moral, and societal commitments.

But as I argued above, the truth value of the virgin birth has been reduced through its overliteralization. Biologically unlikely at best, freakish at worst. Yet some would argue that, unless believers accept it as a physical "miracle," they cannot be considered "orthodox" or genuine Christians. Earlier I contended that limiting its truth value to a biological anomaly actually narrows its powerfully symbolic meaning. Faith professes that Jesus, who was conceived and born as "truly human," represents an inflection point in the unfolding drama of self-consciousness. In Johannine terms, he was born "not of blood, nor of the will of the flesh, nor of the will of man" (John 1:13) but becoming human ("flesh") he has made known the unseen heart of the cosmos.

Gabriel's assurance to the virgin about the Most High's power coming upon and overshadowing her echoes Genesis 1:2. There the *pneuma theou* (rendered both "divine breath" or "mighty wind") moves upon and overshadows the primeval waters. All this prepared for the *logos* (word) that enlightened the darkness. This spirit then becomes the fertilizing agent. As this process was understood prebiologically, a woman only provided a womb for the male seed, here not literal but as mythically conceived. As a servant, or handmaid, Mary becomes the portal through which God's son enters history. This is symbolic narrative, not a biological truth claim.

A "virgin birth," with all its literal contradiction yet metaphorical power, graphically captures this rupture in human self-understanding and historical possibility. In the mythic nature of such a birth, we affirm the equally unlikely emergence of life from the seemingly dead matter of the universe. If we insist that Jesus' birth occurred as a unique physical "miracle" that, by definition, subverts biological laws, we exclude him from the mass of humanity. It reduces his accepting "death, death on a cross" to the equivalent of a Marvel superhero's ruse to fool his opponents. Its literalism limits the symbol's message that human nature itself is *capax dei* (naturally capable of divinity) in the renowned German Jesuit theologian Karl Rahner's formulation.

Rather, as both the "first born son" (Luke 2:7) and the "first born of many brothers and sisters" (Rom 8:29), Jesus reveals in his person the depths of God engendering and dwelling in all of creation. As I argued above, if we limit the meaning of this wonderful (perhaps even feminist) symbol of maternal potency to the cult of sexual virginity, we shrink its truth potential. Even worse, when the story of the virgin birth later morphed into the affirmation that Mary was "ever virgin," it created a sexual ideology that we have outgrown.

The literal belief contravenes a plain reading that the earliest Gospel, Mark, subverts when it tells (very literally!) of his "mother and brothers [even sisters]" coming for Jesus (3:32)—perhaps to pack him up and get him home! Over the centuries, this exaggerated "doctrine" has harmed many women and men and produced not a few nutty obsessions. The deeper truth, captured in the later version of the Creed, that Jesus is "true God and true human" precludes his coming out of Mary's womb with but a single set of chromosomes. Again, literalism stunts deeper truths that the Creed affirms.

At the same time, believers actually rejoice in professing this wondrous conception and birth precisely because of its strong, mythic force. As a poetic and symbolic truth, it does not require adopting a religious ideology that reduces its veracity to its literal, biological force. The virgin birth "says" far more than any gynecological examination of Mary of Nazareth would reveal. Its power lies in its artistry, beauty, and wonder. As I noted earlier, the angel Gabriel's annunciation to the unmarried Mary has given rise to some of the most sublime painted canvases in Western art, as well as to the East's luminous icons. Its visual portrayal ranks with Mary's *Magnificat*, a lyrical poetic text that itself has spawned extraordinary musical settings. Ironically, Mary's song about God's lifting up "the lowly to high places" and sending "the rich empty away" has *not* been taken literally enough. Had it been, the poor might have been valued and treated as Jesus himself treated them. As a religious truth, Mary's unique role elevates womanhood itself as a pregnant text that subverts many of the mores in male-dominated societies, both then and since.

He descended into hell . . .
His death was no ruse. He shared mortality to its fullest.

The second element of the mythic story of Jesus follows his dying on the cross. This element, the *descensus ad inferos*, reflects the ancient three-tiered understanding of the cosmos: the heavens above, the earth between, and hell/hades/sheol below. These last names variously describe the realm of the shades, the fate of dead souls, or the abode of the evil one. In this context, "hell" vividly pictures the mortal fate that awaits us all—death itself that wields its threat to obliterate the living and their share in the goodness of creation.

Following Jesus' death on the cross, his "descent" makes plain that his crucifixion was no show-death, no ruse to escape the fate of all human beings. It corresponds to the poetry cited by St. Paul in his letter to the Philippians about the depth of Christ Jesus' *kenosis* or humility: "even suffering death—death on a cross." Yet some followers in the early Jesus movement (how the early "church" is referred to by social historians today) found this aspect of the drama abhorrent. Eventually known as "Docetists," they professed that Jesus was just the "appearance" of God, not an actual human. In this way, they avoided "the scandal of the cross" by which a divine person suffered the ultimate human fate. This idea would later allow the Qur'an to accept that Jesus was replaced on the cross where he did not die. Rather, like Elijah, he was taken up to heaven so that he could return as God's final messenger of the end time.

But, in mythic terms, the "descent into hell" enacts Jesus' own parable: he is the stronger one awaited by the Baptist who "entering the strong man's house . . . restrained him and plundered his house"—the house of the dead (Mark 3:27). Likewise, Paul claimed that in crucifying Jesus, the "rulers of this world" (1 Cor 2:8) displayed their power over life and death. But, wondrously, God-in-Christ, in death, laid claim to "the spirits in prison" (1 Pet 3:19) whom he revealed to be alive in God.

This scenario was later expanded mythically into "the harrowing of hell," so central to Eastern Christian iconography. In it, Christ is portrayed as binding the devil and looting the underworld of its dead. As Paul wrote in Romans 14: Christ died and lived again "that he might be Lord of both the dead and the living" (v. 9). Here, as well as in Ephesians 4, Christ's cosmic journey into hell undoes the world's alienation from its Creator and crosses the abyss that was said to separate the living from the dead. As mythic scenarios, these images express faith that the lives of all—past, present, and to come—have their origin and their end in God's creative love. The scenes come to us from a physically naïve world. Yet they challenge believers psychologically and spiritually to see their own lives woven into the fabric of space-time beyond how we normally see ourselves living and dying.

On the third day, he arose again from the dead . . .

Post-Calvary, Jesus' fate was seen through the lens of a growing expectation of a future vindication of the just. No longer a single individual, Jesus lives "by the power of God" in a creation being renewed by his Spirit.

The descent, then, only prepares the way for the next, even more startling, affirmation. As Paul to the Corinthians made clear, faith rises or falls on whether Christ is "raised from the dead." But, as suggestive and descriptive as Paul's witness to Christ's risen life is, he never explains what this "rising again" means in literal terms. And neither he nor the Gospels allow us to reduce this "rising" to the resuscitation of a dead corpse that, zombie-like, emerges from the tomb. Later artworks captured the event in such images, but the Gospels' narratives of the "empty tomb" prescind from any literal description of the physical miracle of Jesus' emergence. Frankly, Paul's writings about Christ's being revealed to him and the Gospels' resurrection narratives barely overlap at all. So we need to look at these witnesses as they both compare and contrast.

The Easter Sunday narratives about the empty tomb all post-date Paul's autobiographical narrative of meeting "the Lord." They also differ among themselves in significant details, only agreeing that some followers of Jesus came to the tomb at dawn on the day after the Sabbath (all call this "the third day"). Each of them comprises legendary attempts to ground the meaning of Christ's post-crucifixion fate in events as *they might have been experienced by identifiable persons* among his followers. Paul himself recounts visionary experiences of Christ alive and those of other witnesses whom he names and then numbers at about five hundred (1 Cor 15:6–8).

But these recognition events have little relationship to the stories about Jesus' missing body. In fact, all of these "empty tomb" stories were meant to illustrate for second- or third-generation communities what was meant by knowing Christ and the power of his resurrection. They all supply concrete details of place and time to flesh out imaginatively the belief that the crucified Jesus now "lives by the power of God" (2 Cor 13:4). But all the wonderful details—the young man clothed in white, the one or two angel messengers ("He is not here!"), the earthquake, the sleeping guards, the folded clothes—dramatize an "event" whose full meaning escapes specific places, characters, or exact times.

Each of the evangelists fleshed out their narrative pictures quite differently. Their legendary-like features variously reflected the impact of Jesus' risen life in their communities. Mark's original ending paints a blank screen while hinting at a future appearance in Galilee; Matthew embroiders his new-age depiction with stories of the dead arising at the crucifixion but waiting until Jesus rose to announce themselves. His drama of the Jewish authorities' panicked visit to Pilate and their buying the guards' silence corresponds to his ongoing argument with "the [so-called] scribes and Pharisees" (cf. Matt 23:13). Then he staged a reunion in Galilee at which Jesus does not depart, but assures his followers of his presence with them until the final redo of creation.

Luke crafts the supper at Emmaus with its presaging of Christian liturgy of word and sacred meal as well. He then adds an assurance of Jesus' physical presence at another meal to avoid the inference that he was a ghost. Then the Fourth Gospel's Easter night appearance and its tale of doubting Thomas is combined with the pouring out of the Spirit on the disciples—anticipating Luke's post-ascension reception of this gift. But the evangelists' artistry lies precisely in their diverse efforts to flesh out a reality that escaped any one author's ability to capture how God-in-Christ was both no longer in the flesh but also present in power, a presence soon to be named as the Spirit of the risen Lord.

All of the four Gospels' highly creative narratives reflect earlier, more materialist notions of how God would restore and redeem Israel from its oppressors. Ezekiel's vision of reconstructed bodies rising from their graves and Second Maccabees's assurance that God would re-create the martyrs' bodies as a reward for their faithfulness populated the imaginative world of first-century Jews. We know that, while the Saducean aristocracy denied this developing belief, the early rabbis seized upon it to affirm God's faithfulness. Unlike other beliefs that the "souls of the just" live with God, "resurrection" meant a very this-worldly living again. Belief in a future resurrection became the narrative store of myth that expressed hope, despite desperate political situations, that God would "do a new thing" (Isa 43:19) and restore Israel's freedom and peace. Likewise, the anti-temple Qumran community read the prophets Daniel and Ezekiel in the same vein: God's faithfulness meant renewed life for the martyred just.

But Paul's earlier description of this work of God was not at all dependent on any of the Gospels' Easter accounts. For him, Jesus was "the first-born of those who have fallen asleep," manifested as God's Son in the Spirit in his life beyond death. Unlike the evangelists, his more mythic, pictorial scenarios of resurrection portray a future, cosmic event, not an isolated past event only occurring "on the third day." In the now of belief, Christ lives by the power of God as the Son who was "revealed" to Saul, later named Paul, to become an apostle (Gal 1:16).

His evidence for this new reality manifests itself in his and others' direct experience of the Spirit of the risen Jesus, both ecstatic and otherwise. For him, Christ's risen "body" is the *ekklesia*, the community of faithful called out from both Jews and Gentiles as the forerunner of the new creation. When Christ returns to overcome death as the human condition, resurrection will involve a whole new shape to an individual's self. Paul's mystical vision of the "end" seems much like Jesus' own from the prophet Daniel's vision of the Son of Man receiving dominion from "the Ancient One."

The apostle envisions resurrection as only the first act of a drama that concludes when the Son assumes a subordinate place in the new creation so that "God becomes all in all" (1 Cor 15:28). Though Paul never abandons this earlier mythic scenario of the just coming to life again, he increasingly understands life in Christ as involving a whole new way of living in the brief "now" before the full revelation of Christ through which God is at one again with all creation. Because the Creed later affirms "resurrection" a second time, not as part of a past, but of a future event, I will seek to engage its deeper symbolic meaning in my later pages.

He ascended into heaven . . .

Mythic pictures of ascent and descent represent the means by which the breach between divinity and humanity becomes healed. Christ represents the crossing of that distance once and for all.

Extending the Narrative

The Gospels' mythic scenarios of how the Father was "redeeming" or winning back creation into union with Godself is filled out, first, by the belief that Jesus returned to the divine realm whence he came but also that he remains in the midst of his own. But, as before, briefly examining the differences in the Gospel accounts will be instructive. For as prominent as "ascension" appears in the Creed, only one of the four Gospels (supplemented by Luke, vol. 2, or The Acts of the Apostles) supplies us with anything like a heavenly exit from *terra firma*. What is explicit in Luke remains (at best) implicit and unexpressed in Matthew, though his final scene (Matt 28:16–20) has often been as the equivalent of Luke's ascension. In fact, both represent very different expansions of the earlier (unexpanded) version of Mark.

Two subsequent endings sought to bring Mark into line with the later Synoptic Gospels. And the longer of these two additions (16:9–20) captures some of Luke's post-resurrection appearances, adding some signs (snake handling!) that believers are said to be able to accomplish. Cobbling together a commissioning "to all the world" with Jesus being "taken up into heaven" (Mark 16:19), the "longer ending" makes an editorial effort to rectify Matthew and Luke's divergent final scenes.[23]

Matthew's concluding tableau occurs on a mountain in Galilee where the disciples have regathered—as Jesus instructed the women to tell them to do (Mark 16:7/Matt 28:10). But Luke stages his scene around Bethany outside Jerusalem. Rather than Jesus "withdrawing from them" and being carried up into heaven (Luke 24:51), Matthew claimed, as noted earlier, that Jesus told his disciples that he was remaining with them "until the end of the age" (v. 20). So in Matthew, Jesus does not depart into heaven, but remains present "wherever two or three are gathered" (18:20). Like the Fourth Gospel, where Jesus the eternal Word-made-flesh returns to the Father, he also remains an active presence as his Spirit continues to save the world through God's love.

---

23. The editors of the New Revised Standard Version (NT 74) noted that these endings indicate "that different attempts were made to provide a suitable ending for the Gospel."

But what Matthew and Luke do share are various commissions to Jesus' disciples detailing their tasks during the in-between time, the age of the church. Matthew specifies "preach to all the nations, baptizing them," while in Luke they are to "preach repentance" and forgiveness "to all the nations." But only Luke accompanied his mission-sending by then adding the fleshed-out scenario in his next volume (Acts 1:9). There Jesus is "taken out of their sight" on a cloud. Having now achieved a unique communion with the Father, he would one day return "in the same way as you saw him go into heaven" (v. 11). A vibrant picture to be sure—artists, iconographers, and illuminators East and West knew as much.

But in Luke alone, "heaven" and its clouds equate with the sky/the heavens (the *shamayim* of Genesis 1:1). Picturing the "clouds of heaven" as a means of transport may well have stemmed from the same text cited by Jesus at his trial before the Sanhedrin: the coming of the Son of Man on the clouds from Daniel 7:14. But Matthew, again, differs. In his Gospel, "heaven," in the singular, is a metaphor for the Divine Name as well as for the mythic abode of God, but is not reached by clouds. In that realm, which Jesus proclaimed had come near (4:17) bringing the will of God to earth (Matt 6:10), "heaven" only derivatively names a place of dwelling. The meaning more properly describes a state of Being-in-God.

So the truth value of the "ascension" does not rely on the narrative claim that Jesus became a space traveler. (Any more than Mary's "assumption" means that she rode on a cloud to heaven before or after she had fallen asleep surrounded by the apostles, as later legend would have it.) "He ascended into heaven" straddles the paradox that Jesus of Nazareth left this world in death but, as the Christ of God, remains in the world as "his body," the church, through the life-giving power of God's Spirit. In mythic terms, a post-resurrection "ascension" unites his earthly mortality with his heavenly origin in a great act of divine/human reconciliation. As both "the first born of all creation" and "the first born from the dead," Jesus has become a cosmic figure uniting God's fullness with the "body" that is the church. By doing so, he reconciles "all things, whether on earth or in heaven" (Col 1:20). Mystical statements, for

Extending the Narrative

sure, but how else were first-century Christians able to capture the stunning unity between God and humanity that the story of Christ reveals? Aliens no longer, we are still mining these outsized affirmations as we contemplate and strive to achieve humanity's difficult reconciliation of different, often hostile, "tribes and tongues, peoples and nations." The only reason believers can do either lies in this affirmation: "earth" and "heaven" name, not two, but one realm where the justice of God resides (2 Pet 2:13), in promise if not yet in actuality.

And sits at the right hand of the Father . . .

As the New Adam, Christ's enthronement represents the full reunion of the Creator with humanity.

Similarly, Christ's enthronement at the right hand of the Father constitutes a powerful mythic image portraying a mortal human being as "God's right-hand man" (to be sexist!). Redeemed humanity, in the person of the risen/exalted Christ, is firmly ensconced alongside and in communion with the Originating Love "in which we live and move and have our being" (Acts 17:28). Death no longer has the last word, committing those who have died to sheol, the land of the dead. This threefold narrative of *resurrection-ascension-enthronement* creates a marvelous pictorial triptych. But, as a single movement, it captures the drama that began in Genesis and will extend beyond even Revelation's hallucinatory crises that beset humanity in an as yet unredeemed world. All of these diverse biblical screenplays envision a future in which a restored humanity dwells in unmediated union with God who has "made new" all of creation (Rev 21:5, echoing Isa 66:22).

For Christians, that mystery, or revealed vision for creation, took flesh in the birth, life, work, and martyr's death of Jesus of Nazareth, a Jewish man of the first century of the Common Era. Portrayed variously as Son, Lord, Messiah/Christ, the Stronger One, Word, Lamb of God, Living Water, Bread of Life, The Good

This I Believe

Shepherd, Vine, I Am, Victim, King, Priest, Master, and Lord, Jesus' identity can only be grasped through poetic expression. Replacing myth, poetry, and symbol with conceptual dogmas and doctrines can often diminish their power and their truth value. Once again, all these names and titles are metaphors that, by definition, make their way around the reality in question, circling its center, but never naming the Unnamed in any uncontested, literally exact manner.[24]

They all struggle to express a Communion between the cosmos and its Generating Force, made real through the mystery of the restored life of Jesus, "the first born of many brothers and sisters" (Rom 8:29 in NRSV: "of a large family"). Metaphor assures that verbal expression, which the Greek fathers called *kataphasis*, can never prevail over the *apophasis* (or unspokenness) of religious experience.[25] Symbols hold the two in tension as strangely coincident. Without the necessary humility in the face of the Ineffable, religion descends into ideology, a lifeless system of obligatory adherence.

All of these elaborate, narrative scenarios are only grasped as *pictures*, symbols of imagined physical realities that escape any impoverished literal interpretation. God does not live "in heaven above," but that's how many people since antiquity have expressed the realm of the Transcendent. Hence, the language of communion between the divine and the human has naturally followed a descent/ascent pattern between heaven and earth at least as far back as Jacob's vision of the ladder (Gen 28:12). Verbal pictures, images, tableaux, and visionary scenarios have been, and will continue to be, unavoidable tools that religion takes advantage of to express what is ultimately unspeakable—the Mystery at the center of existence. But ascribing their truth value to what they literally

---

24. On metaphor, see Weil, who claims, "The metaphor of the 'veil' or the 'reflection' applied by the mystics to faith enable them . . . to accept the Church's teaching, not as truth, but as something behind which the truth is to be found" (*Letter*, 23).

25. Armstrong asks whether "the growing appreciation of the limitations of human knowledge . . . give rise to a new kind of apophatic theology?" (*Case for God*, 317).

describe impoverishes their ability to engage humans, with their limited sight, in realms and truths beyond our immediate grasp.

From there he will come to judge the living and the dead . . .

A victim of injustice has become the agent of a very different standard of God's reconciling justice: to pray the Creed today commits a believer to "do justice" across the board.

This threefold drama of ascent is now complemented by yet another mythic scenario: this one of descent and judgment. Ideas, as well as images of the final judgment, also known as the great assize, have created some of the most compelling, yet misleading, conceptual beliefs in the annals of Christianity. Many of the most famous artists and iconographers have found them impossible to resist. Musicians, as well, gravitate to the thundering and ominous words of the medieval (not biblical) *dies irae*, "day of wrath, that dreadful day."

These visions of judgment and a final reckoning for injustices, fueled by the book of Revelation and others, have sought to rattle people's complacency about the moral implications of their lives. They make a strong case that words and deeds, personally, socially, and even cosmic-historically, count. But these frightful, apocalyptically tinged scenarios end up turning divine judgment into the ultimate carrot and stick. They miss the forest through the trees; their real content is obscured by the vividness of their depiction.

In truth, the Creed's notion of judgment can shift in a more truthful direction if we take into account a masterful twist that appears in Jesus' parable of the sheep and the goats in Matthew 25. In this parable, two scenarios have been merged: first, the descent of the Son of Man (again, see Daniel 7 for this generating image); the second, a royal courtroom, the normal venue for justice to be dispensed in the ancient world. A great separation is pending, here as pastorally envisioned, between the sheep (rewarded) and the goats (punished). But something more basic than reward or punishment is at work here. For the nations' peoples all experience the same shocking surprise. Both those judged just and those who showed themselves unjust equally mistake how much this king/judge operates against type.

Unlike those whom Jesus, in another place, calls the rulers and great ones who lord it over their own, this royal judge essentially identifies with the victims of humanity's indifference. He judges himself to be united as one with the homeless, the naked, the imprisoned, the hungry. These "least ones" reveal how the divine nature actually appears among the creatures of earth. This judge, none other than the crucified and risen Lord, rules on cases put before him based on the communion between the lowly and their Savior. The "just" only thought they were "doing the right thing," while the "unjust" merely pursued their own self-interest. But neither group understood how deeply "God . . . loved the world" (John 3:16) so as to become incarnate in suffering humanity.

What starts as a story of impending judgment reveals a more intimate criterion of justice than any elaborate moral or ethical philosophy could articulate. The Creed's story of a crucified victim reappearing as humanity's judge undoes normal standards of moral obligation as Jesus himself observed: Even the tax collectors love those who love them! (Matt 5:45). It also reveals that what we term "charity" does not measure up to the loftier demands of justice. On the issue of judgment, Paul denied that, for "those who are in Christ Jesus," who operate according to the "law of the Spirit" (Rom 8:1), condemnation is ever a threat. But here, Jesus' parable illustrates the "surpassing justice" (Matt 5:20) urged on his disciples, one that outstrips any merely legal obligation.[26] The story it tells burrows into the weightier issues of moral and religious law:

---

26. The characterization of what Jesus calls for is my own, based on the plain sense of the text of Matt 5:20 ("For I tell you, unless your righteousness exceeds that of the scribes and Pharisees, you will never enter the kingdom of heaven"). When the so-called "antitheses" follow (5:21–48), it is clear that what Jesus stipulates about this righteousness/justice exceeds any earlier conception of it.

"justice and mercy and faith" (Matt 23:23), not compliance under threat of punishment.

The truth value, worthy of our faith-profession in these images of reward and punishment, is found beyond the mesmerizing attraction of apocalypse, disaster, or reward. Can we, then, affirm "judgment" within the scope of biblical faith without understanding it as God's raising the threat level to DEFCON 5? Is it possible to relate to divine judgment in any but the naïve sense that God's a "hanging judge" ready to convict us on even the flimsiest of charges? I think we can, but only if we understand the metaphors of judge and judgment as Jesus developed them on the basis of a prophetic call to covenant responsibility.

As best we can make out, Jesus' own consciousness of judgment arose from the Old Testament/Hebrew Scriptures' conviction that "chosenness" means intimacy. Israel's God had entered into a *ketubah*, a marriage contract, that called both parties to faithfulness. When that covenant was broken, God's messengers, the prophets, arose as mediators/arbitrators to name the injustices and plead for both atonement and forgiveness. (When God was seen as not upholding his end of the bargain, even the Lord could be sued; cf. Jer 12:1 and the litigation in Job 38–41.) Over and over again, the prophets highlighted the sins against widows and orphans, the indebted, the lowly, the stranger or alien. They sued kings, priests, and ordinary people for violations of the covenant. Examples are too numerous to detail here, but the point is that biblical faith, by definition, requires seeking justice, living justly, and establishing justice for the land's afflicted.

In the biblical revelation, *justice* reigns above and matters far beyond "prudence, fortitude, and temperance" (an original pagan quartette of the virtues): justice names the heart of the divine/human relationship. Read Isaiah 1–3; Jeremiah 7; Amos 4; Micah 3, all of which demonstrate how doing justice surpasses cultic worship or any notion of faith as transactional dealmaking. God's justice (also called *righteousness*) equates with salvation, liberation, and redemption, not despite, but because of its character as mercy. God's judgment calls people to act justly, and any notion of punishment has to be seen in the context of motivating people to "straighten up and fly right." Expressions of God's anger—so often pilloried by critics of the Bible—project human frustrations and fears onto a human-shaped idea of divinity. If there were such a God, he/she would have plenty of reasons to be "hot in the nose" (Hebrew for "anger") and to relaunch the mythic flood. But even as a primitive story, it affirms that only a *just* person could reestablish the human lineage (Gen 6:9).

The New Testament doubles down on the prophets' call in the face of the manifest *injustice* of the crucifixion of Jesus. When Christians declared that Jesus would return "to judge the living and the dead," they universalized the covenant relationship that called for doing justice. God's role as "the Judge of all the earth" (Gen 18:25) came out from under its cover as a cosmic or karmic threat. Despite the popularity of the metaphor of final judgment, the meaning of divine judgment has now changed because a victim of injustice, of religious and political expediency, exercises it. In an astonishing role reversal, the teacher of nonviolence, non-retaliation, unmerited mercy, and inexhaustible forgiveness of God becomes the agent who calls us to "do justice" beyond "giving to each according to his/her due" (Aristotle's definition adopted by Aquinas).[27] God's justice in Christ grows in its expansiveness to encompass "the evil and the good . . . the righteous and the unrighteous" (Matt 5:45) who all receive the gifts of God in equal measure.

For his part, Paul joined together sacrificial and judicial imagery in another scandalous twist. He argued that God provided us a model to act for reconciliation and for real justice by refusing to count up humanity's sins as the final arbiter of who deserves mercy (2 Cor 5:18–21). As he would also argue afterwards in Romans, God's justice and God's love, in the face of the crucifixion of the Just One, inverts punishment into forgiveness and reconciliation

---

27. According to this view, justice lies behind the "virtue of religion" by which humans owe God religious worship. The movement does not flow from God to us (as in St. Paul), but from us to God. *Catechism of the Catholic Church*, 2nd ed., 1807.

rather than wrath—either God's or any human societies' version of it (5:18; 11:32).

As a result, I take "justice" to be a stricter rendering of the Bible's Hebrew and Greek terms rather than the alternative "righteousness." To be "right" has other connotations in English, just as to be "righteous" can too easily connote a "self-righteous" person who demands certain moral attitudes and actions of others. God's "righteousness" can be taken to refer to inconvenient or especially overweening moral demands. Whereas God's "justice" (as above) is scandalously inclusive—of both Jews and Gentiles, sinners and obedient, the just and the unjust, male and female, slave and free (dare we say "gay and straight"?).[28] In brief, "to judge the living and the dead" plays upon the historical myth of a coming great assize or final judgment, but the belief transforms the metaphor into a human, flesh-and-blood reality for believers to emulate. As Jesus told the skeptical lawyer in the parable of the merciful, hence just, Samaritan, "Go and do likewise" (Luke 10:37).

Few, if any, human societies and their systems of so-called justice have reached for, let alone adopted, such a standard of justice. Thinner forms of justice settle for punishment rather than healing. We divide societies, groups, and persons into convenient binaries: good or evil, innocent or guilty, often without respect to the inequities and pathologies that bedevil even our best efforts at achieving fairness or impartiality. But society's sins of division only occasion God's justice. They do call for accountability, for righting genuine wrongs, for rebalancing the scales that tilt toward power and wealth.[29] But God's judgment in Christ never rests con-

28. Weil comments, "(Moreover this light and this rain [Matt 5:45] also possess probably a spiritual significance, that is to say, that all—both in Israel and outside it, both the Church and outside it—have grace showered upon them *equally*, although the majority reject it.)" *Letter*, 45.

29. Though Supreme Court Justice Sonia Sotomayor felt it necessary to back away from her earlier statement that a "wise Latina" might render superior judgment to that of a white male who hadn't lived on the margins of society, she was onto something very biblical. The requirement, in her judicial oath, that she "do equal right to the poor and to the rich" is twinned with administering justice "without respect to persons" as if they meant the same thing. They do not, despite most English translations of both the Hebrew and Greek

tent with condemnation or plea bargains that themselves concretize inequality in our courts. The prophets of old looked forward to God's *shalom*, the peace and wholeness that alone fill the measure of real justice. Like them, Paul envisions this as nothing less than the mystery of God's mercy to all.

In his densest effort to work out the implications of the universal gospel that he preached, the apostle figured out what he called a *mysterion* (Rom 11:25–32). God had responded to humanity's universal disobedience and injustice with universal mercy. Immediately after this conclusion, he writes ecstatically over his having uncovered "the depth and the riches of the wisdom and the knowledge of God" (vv. 33–36). But several hundred years later, St. Augustine read these verses as a cry of despair that humans could never know God's counsel. Instead, the apostle was actually proclaiming radical good news for humanity. God's inclusive justice offered human societies a blueprint that few have learned to live by.

The Christ story does not flinch from this bold claim that the deepest form of justice stems from the depths of God's mercy. This story accepts historical contingency and human tragedy, just as it recognizes individuation, free will, and the inevitability of sin. But, beyond all legal requirements or punishment for crimes, the very being of God as Communion argues that grace abounds the more through the outpouring of the Spirit. Hence, love remains "the fulfilling of the law" (Rom 13:8). And law itself must always serve the needs of justice, expansively defined as restoring integrity or wholeness in the torn fabric of the lives of individuals and societies, reconciling opposites rather than resting in our inevitable division. Recovering original justice (as more basic than so-called original sin) allows us, as closely as possible, to act as one with

---

expressions being rendered "no impartiality." "Without respect to persons," in Deut 16:19 (KJV), 2 Chr 19:7, Job 34:19, and even Rom 2:11 (*prosōpolēmpsia*) originally meant countering those who distort judgment and give bribes to judges, hence expect preference. By contrast, God's judgment, by not "respecting [such] persons" turns out to favor those who have been left out; it may even tip the scales back in the direction of the widow and the orphan who can't afford a lawyer.

the life-giving force of creation itself. In the various considerations to follow, I will attempt to articulate how mercy and compassion must shape just responses to a range of vital issues that our local and global societies must face. Without them, justice shrinks to a slogan. Its emblem of the perfectly weighted scales will only continue as a cover-up of the rampant inequality afflicting every portion of humanity today.

Doing Justice Today

The centrality of mercy and compassion means that, if the Christ story reveals any truth to live by, doing justice must lie at the foundation of Christian belief and practice. To profess the Creed means to commit oneself to this overwhelmingly humane ideal and to work against all the forces that divide societies, especially in religion and politics. As I argued earlier, reducing justice to a virtue to be practiced among others by earnest individuals diminishes its fundamental significance.

So let me spell out some of the particular commitments to doing justice that I see as implied by the demands of the Creed today. A number flow from a tradition of articulated "faith and morals" that necessarily develops and cannot remain static. For Catholics, this recognition led the Second Vatican Council to formally change church teaching on religious liberty and the role of conscience, to repudiate anti-Semitism in all its forms, and to admit that truths lie in other religious traditions.

Building on such a dynamic notion of faith response, I wish to describe, first, some forms of doing justice that have received notable and valuable attention, particularly in Christian social teaching. My effort is not comprehensive or definitive. Rather, I mean to provoke reflection on how the creedal affirmation of Christ's being "judge of the living and the dead" carries in its symbolic and mythic shape serious consequences even for those not professing it religiously. I will then follow some more familiar expressions of just practice today with an effort to articulate additional areas that

I believe could benefit from a further process of theological reflection and development.

The first of these is *racial justice* and the repudiation of racism which today has risen to the top of a religious justice agenda. Christianity, at least, has finally reached a stage in its moral maturity that condemned unreservedly any distinction between the essential, God-given dignity of any person based on race or ethnicity. If every human being reflects the "image and likeness of God"—a truth as old as Genesis 1:27—then any "social or cultural discrimination in fundamental personal rights on the grounds of sex, race, color, social conditions, language, or religion must be curbed and eradicated as incompatible with God's design."[30]

Based on this stated belief, repairing the long-lasting damage done by systemic racism makes a vital claim on believing Christians. Justice requires making whole what has been torn apart, restoring equality that has been denied, making restitution for what has been stolen. Decades ago, when some Black activists began to advocate for the United States to make financial reparations to the descendants of enslaved Africans, few seemed to take the proposal seriously. The intervening years, as well as serious research and soul-searching, have continued to strengthen the case for reparations.

Denied equal civil rights, access to sources of stable employment, and wealth accumulation, or subjected to theft of property, discriminatory housing, and inferior educational opportunities, they possess a valid claim to be compensated for the generational poverty and deprivation these practices have caused. Justice that does not work for restoration and reconciliation, or that holds separate those whom God equally loves, cannot pretend to embody the biblical summons to righteousness. Reduced to personal fairness or compassionate acts that ignore our communal responsibility for those who are "other" yet one-with-us, justice empties itself of any substance.

---

30. *Catechism of the Catholic Church*, 1935, quoting Vatican II, *Gaudium et Spes*, 29.

Extending the Narrative

This moves *economic justice* as an essential component of *social justice* into the forefront of our consideration. Advocates of both have consistently called out the sins of unrestrained market-based capitalism as well as any forced collectivism. Yet too many pious Christians bracket challenges to the so-called free market, avoiding gospel-based demands to hear the cry of the poor as "politics" and, hence, open to self-interested dispute. Among other faith leaders, Pope Francis, totally in accord with his predecessors, cited the injustices that occur when short-term financial gain (read "shareholder value") is the bottom line. Allowing it to dominate any accurate impact assessment of economic decisions on persons, especially those on the margins of society, has become today's "golden calf." As an advocate of the mercy that inhabits just economic policies, he calls us to "reject a magical conception of the market, which would suggest that problems can be solved simply by an increase in the profits of companies or individuals."[31] Reliance on "market forces," with no consideration of their often-devastating impact on the poor of the world, deserves to be rated as "sin" as much as an individual act of theft.

Unjust societies pay little or no attention to *ecological/environmental justice*, which connects the struggle to combat poverty and restore dignity to the excluded with protecting the natural world from the devastation that consumerism has wrought. The same world-historical papal encyclical, citing the ecumenical patriarch of Constantinople and other religious leaders, calls for nothing less than "ecological conversion" that Francis declares to be "not an optional or a secondary aspect of our Christian experience."[32] Here, creedal faith calls for "the rubber to hit the road" and for serious lifestyle changes to be made. Economists such as Marianna Mazzucato, the author of *Mission Economy: A Moonshot Guide to Changing Capitalism,* clearly spell out some of the changes that twenty-first-century, developed societies must make for self-preservation, if not for living a just life.

---

31. Francis, *Laudato Si',* 190.
32. Francis, *Laudato Si',* 217.

This I Believe

At this point, I have outlined some of the well-known branches that grow directly from the rooted tree of justice. But we are not done trying to mine the extent that mercy and compassion are its fruit. Yet, as our grasp of the truths of the Creed continue to grow and develop "until we all attain to the unity of the faith . . . to maturity, to the full measure of the full stature of Christ" (Eph 4:13), we can't stop at obvious applications of just practice. For, in recent years, genuine new growth has taken place, and I will venture spelling out these new fields. My expansive sketch of justice today may scandalize some readers and risk a harsh, even scathing, judgment. But, if "the truth is one,"[33] we must venture as far outside faith's comfort zone as God's inclusive justice calls for us to go.

Rising today onto many Christians' moral radar, *restorative justice* has begun to challenge and seek reform of what we have formerly been content to call "criminal justice." This new perspective has arisen from several sources. No one who understands the impact of the inequity in educational resources, housing opportunities, and family stability, which run straight along the lines of ethnicity and race, doubts that crime follows poverty as the night follows the day. Many upstanding citizens remain content to "let the punishment fit the crime" without scrutinizing either the wells from which much criminal behavior arises or the negative outcomes of our "correctional" systems themselves.

Of course, not all jails or prisons are created or managed equally. Some offer rehabilitative services such as drug programs, higher education, arts programs, and violence prevention. Many others seem content just to lock up and mistreat the poor. Revelations, such as provided in Bryan Stevenson's *Just Mercy*, Michelle Alexander's *The New Jim Crow: Mass Incarceration in the Age of Colorblindness*, or Anthony Ray Hinton's *The Sun Does Shine: How I Found Life and Freedom on Death Row*, have had some success in opening the eyes of the blind to the discriminatory intent with which penal systems have treated people in different racial

---

33. Rohr, (November 22, 2016), The Perennial Tradition, https://cac.org/truth-is-one-2016-11-22/.

groups.[34] "White-collar crime" connotes a lot more than financial shenanigans of people in offices.

Beyond these (now well-known) instances of judicial inequity, restorative justice asks when and how should we consider that "justice is done." Certainly not when the legal system of administering justice only knows the binary choice, guilty or innocent, losing or winning, incarceration or freedom. Meeting violent crime with violent punishment, inhuman acts with inhumane jails and prisons, violations of personal safety with deprivation of dignity fails any real test of biblical justice as I am struggling to articulate it.

Horrendous crime and established guilt are real. But an "eye for an eye" mentality has allowed thousands of persons (mostly of color) to be unjustly convicted and sent to languish in prison. Once "inside," they are often subjected to abuse, inadequate nutrition, substandard health care, and living conditions that strip them of any dignity. Above all, this mentality leads politicians, who demonize the incarcerated and claim that they "deserve what they get," to sturdily support society's right to end an incarcerated person's life.

Today, a growing religious, as well as secular, consensus has begun to turn its back on the death penalty even in capital cases. The democracies in the European Union have long since done this. In this country, public consciousness has begun to grasp the legacy of the Jim Crow South's racist slave-labor system in today's unequal application of drug laws against Black and Brown persons. Case after case of incarcerating the poor and often innocent in the name of "swift justice" have revealed that harsh sentencing requirements, devoid of even the concept of mercy, actually pervert justice rather than uphold it. When Sr. Helen Prejean published

---

34. The excesses against and struggles for equal justice in the nation's penal systems have been highlighted by the Marshall Project (themarshallproject.org), a nonpartisan, nonprofit news organization that seeks to create and sustain a sense of national urgency about the US criminal justice system. It seeks to have an impact on the system through journalism, rendering it more fair, effective, transparent, and humane.

Dead Man Walking,[35] she boosted the moral campaign that has begun to undo the skein of reasons used to justify state-sponsored murder. Recently, Pope Francis has emended the official teaching of the Catholic Church, removing previous exceptions that saw capital punishment as acceptable. Restorative justice calls out the need to create alternatives to incarceration, a movement for which people of faith should advocate loudly. Inhuman conditions in prisons and the lack of serious efforts to rehabilitate/heal both nonviolent and violent offenders make our pretensions to "liberty and justice for all" a farcical charade.

Restorative justice, as both an idea and a practice, seeks to foster accountability for crime, care for victims, and civil well-being in the administration of our criminal and civil law systems. As such, the movement represents an application of what the judgment/justice of Christ means in the twenty-first century of our era. One recent study makes the case for this view of justice that reflects Christian belief in forgiveness, resurrection, and reconciliation of all involved.

> [R]estorative justice is about righting a wrong not only for victims but also for offenders and communities. It is about making amends rather than punishment, restitution rather than retribution. In criminal justice, [restorative justice] is about healing individuals, communities, and even nations after harm caused from wrongdoing ...[36]

As someone who has taught higher education classes in a maximum security correctional facility, I know that when dignity, education, and care accompany incarceration, even formerly violent persons, serving years for their crimes, can become forces for good. They act as catalysts for change among fellow incarcerated people, and then they continue to do so in their communities

---

35. Her 1993 book was later made into a well-received film that garnered an Oscar for Best Actress (Susan Sarandon) and other nominations in 1995. Both an opera by Jake Heggie (2000) and a play by Tim Robbins (2002) have been based upon it.

36. Van Wormer and Walker, *Restorative Justice*, xv–xvi.

when they are released. Both as students in correctional facilities and as released graduates, they have an outsized impact through their degreed professional work, on their home communities, and on the public's imagination of ex-cons (a term I use regretfully).

A few years back, at a privately funded college graduation ceremony, a prominent philanthropist was taking in the impact of educational accomplishment on the new graduates, their families, and their children in attendance. She made this observation for the record: "I've taught Sunday school for years. But, you know what, *this* is redemption!" A simple statement that made a profound theological point, one grounded in Jesus' echoing the Servant of Isaiah's vocation to "proclaim release" to the poor, the blind, the oppressed, and the captives" (Luke 4:18). At root, "redemption" means "buying back/restoring" life and dignity. Or, as Jesus described his own mission, "The healthy do not need a physician; sick people do. I have not come to call the just, but sinners" (Mark 2:17). In the end, reducing justice to retribution, or "getting even" being the best revenge, only elevates power over right, force over persuasion, punishment over conversion.

At this juncture, I wish to extend this treatment of restorative justice to argue that it lies firmly in the clear teaching of Jesus on non-retaliation. For that teaching establishes a more basic rationale for restorative, rather than merely retributive, justice than our sad history of injustices alone might make today. I find it, first, in the clear teaching of Paul in Romans (12:17–21). A second instance sits brightly in the sermon of Jesus that Matthew stages on "the Mount" (5:38–48). Luke's similar version occurs when Jesus descends to the plain to teach (6:27–36).

Initially, Paul's seems the more strategic of these. When counseling his audience not to "repay evil for evil," he cites the possibility that living peaceably with all might be conditional, i.e., "so far as it depends on you . . ." (v. 18). But he then falls back on the Law against vengeance (Lev 19:18), which properly is God's business (Deut 32:35), before citing Solomon's wisdom from Proverbs. In essence, treat your enemies kindly as it will "heap burning coals on their heads" (25:21–22)—a metaphor for sure, but one that seeks to use an adversary's embarrassment to one's own advantage. This strategy for overcoming evil with good (12:21) counsels subverting, rather than opposing, the evildoer. It is a strategy that Matthew's Jesus makes more explicit yet.

When confronting forms of violence/crime yet avoiding standard forms of redress, Jesus advocated a range of subversive strategies. In the last century, Gandhi himself mirrored such nonviolent modes of action. Faced with violent oppression, he had a "clear sighted acceptance of the necessity to use . . . the presence of evil as a fulcrum for good and for liberation."[37] At no time did Jesus, any more than Gandhi, understand non-retaliation, or the "truth" of nonviolence, to require passive acceptance of evil—or crime. Instead, they both seemed to grasp that evil acts in themselves contain their own punishments. As evil, they should provoke a believer's mercy and compassion as the best strategy for overcoming them.[38]

For example, when considering the law of *talion*, "an eye for an eye and a tooth for a tooth," a blow to the face for a blow to the face, Jesus opts for other than the "in-kind" justice enshrined in many ancient law codes (Matt 5:38-39). Originally these laws functioned as a check on retaliatory violence that was often a familial or social duty to avenge wrong. To demand that the person who caused an injury suffer an equal one had the effect of limiting the counterclaims of the one wronged: i.e., one could not condemn to death an adversary for an injury that did not result in death. But Jesus lived in a society with developed systems of law (both Jewish and Roman) where gross, physical redress was, by and large, regulated. Replacing vengeance with a system of legal redress or torts still retains an adversarial, if not antagonistic, premise. Going to court guaranteed the same binary choice we face today: one party wins and the other loses.

---

37. Merton, ed., *Gandhi*, 11.
38. Merton, ed., quoting Thomas Aquinas (*Summa Theologica* II, IIae, q. 30, art. 1, ad. 1 and art. 2) on sin deserving mercy and forgiveness in place of anger and punishment (*Gandhi*, 12).

Extending the Narrative

By contrast, the "surpassing justice" of the kingdom calls on the plaintiff to turn the other cheek, give the coat as well, and walk the extra mile. These admonitions represent three responses to aggression, personal, social/legal, and political, that people before and since have faced. All three strategically subvert purely antagonistic relationships and promote non-coercion in order to invite the adversary into a relationship of equality and harmony. The earlier effort at equity in the law of *talion*, for all its good intentions, no longer meant much in social or political systems where the rich and powerful play by their own rules. Jesus sought to level the playing field, giving "victims" a peacemaking power to act in their own favor *as well as* in favor of an adversary.

The third of these strategies ("walk the extra mile") takes on a clarity because we know its background in the Roman armies' occupation of Judea and its neighbors. As demonstrated in the scene in Matthew 27:32 where the soldiers "compel" Simon of Cyrene to carry Jesus' cross, any legionnaire had the power to "impress" ordinary citizens. Anyone tagged by an occupier would have to perform manual labor that the soldier shunned. When confronted with this humiliation, Jesus advised that his followers *seem* to submit (not unlike when one "turns the other cheek" or "gives your coat as well"). But, once what is demanded is done, Jesus' strategy would turn the "victim" into the oppressor's benefactor. By "walking the extra mile," the walker reestablishes a relationship of equality, subverting the soldier's assertion of superior status. Neither party is finally demeaned; the victim no longer an inferior and the oppressor now the recipient of a favor.

The final challenge/affirmation that Jesus then delivered ("love your enemies," 5:44) makes the strategy of loving subversion explicit. It reveals how much Jesus understood the law to love your neighbor as yourself ("the greatest commandment," cf. 22:34–40) to expand into hostile territory, as it were. The distinction between those who one was required to love and those you might well despise was a constant in recent history from the period of the Maccabees through the Roman occupation. By commanding a "surpassing justice" that loved one's enemies and prayed for one's persecutors, Jesus meant to broaden his followers' "circle of concern,"[39] their capacity for loving more than just their own, for calling people "neighbor" who would normally remain strangers in an antagonistic social and political relationship.

Our inherited tradition that justice is done when an offender is punished falls far short of the Sermon's summons to justice. The radical reinterpretation that results reminds us that, in situations of conflict between opposing goods (i.e., the safety of the community vs. accountability for crime or evildoing), "the left side of the brain, with its usual application of conventional thinking, is ground to a halt." But facing such conflicts creatively "forces the right side of the brain into gear, seeking intuitive, unconventional answers so that action can be renewed with greater purpose."[40]

By analogy, Jesus was the incarnation of the right side of the brain! His solutions to impasse situation and conflicts (e.g., paying taxes to Caesar, losing a sheep, the prodigal father, the woman caught in adultery) were unconventional to an amazing degree. So unconventional that Christians call them revelation—even when they fail to follow them. They remind us of the words of Isaiah the prophet:

> As high as the heavens are above the earth
> so high are my ways above your ways,
> my thoughts above your thoughts (55:9).

In other words, when Christians confront the collapse of traditional systems of behavior, when old moral norms prove too weak, or when fresh insight is needed to break a moral or political impasse which seems insoluble, the surpassing justice called for in the Sermon on the Mount can shed some light on our darkened imaginations. God's justice, as Jesus lived it, flows from the

---

39. Martha Nussbaum outlines an allied scenario when she writes, "If distant people and abstract principles are to get a grip on our emotions, therefore, these emotions must somehow position themselves within our circle of concern, creating a sense of 'our' life in which these people and events matter as part of 'us,' our own flourishing. For this movement to take place, symbols and poetry are crucial" (*Political Emotions*, 11).

40. Lane, "Spirituality and Political Commitment," 197.

Extending the Narrative

Creator's love for his creatures. It summons us to radical acts of shared humanity, the very foundation stone of restorative justice. He incarnated the nondiscriminatory love of the Creator and invited his followers to adopt unselfish love and nonviolent action for justice as the hallmark of their response to the crises of their own times.

Another branch of the tree that has begun to sprout more prominently of late I will call *gender justice*. For many Christians, this has been a long and rocky growing season. Yet, as early as the widely acclaimed 1963 letter *Pacem in Terris* ("Peace on Earth"), Pope John XXIII cited the changing role of women in society as one of the "signs of the times" that believers needed to recognize. As he wrote,

> Women are gaining an increasing awareness of their natural dignity. Far from being content with a purely passive role or allowing themselves to be regarded as a kind of instrument, they are demanding both in domestic and in public life the rights and duties which belong to them as human persons.[41]

But, in the years since, among other bodies, the Catholic Church has struggled with the implications of this "sign." But it clearly begins with recognizing the full equality all human beings before any sexual differentiation comes into play. In evolutionary terms, male and female genders developed as an alternative to (and definite improvement upon) asexual reproduction, which still occurs in some simple organisms. In requiring two different sets of genes combining to produce even a single-celled organism, nature hit upon a scheme that creates an infinite variety of unique beings. It also amounts to a strategy to outfox our coevolving antagonists, the viruses! All individuals resemble their progenitors but emerge as distinct from them.

Throughout history, most human cultures have accepted this functional strategy for assuring a more robust gene line. They mostly developed incest taboos to discourage mating too

---

41. John XXIII, *Pacem in Terris*, 41.

This I Believe

closely within an extended family. But many have also taken up the gender-differentiation ball and run with it. Differentiating the male from the female of the species hardened into a fortress for male privilege and preference. Gender became more than a relative distinction that helped shape an individual's personal identity. Rather, cultures and societies have absolutized this gender binary in some harmful ways. The functional differences between males and females, particularly regarding birth and child-rearing, went from biological descriptions to being declared divine mandates.[42]

"Male and female God created them" has served for centuries, not as originally meant to picture the divine image in humans, but as a rigid distinction written in divine law. Absolutizing male and female, via their physical characteristics, then led to a rigid social construction of gender as destiny. Nature's random distribution of sex genes, something only recently understood, could be ignored and even outlawed. As a result, some persons with biologically male features do not experience themselves as they appear outwardly. The same is true for biologically female persons whose inner life defies their outward appearance. Today we know that nature distributes male, female, and gender-neutral characteristics along a sliding scale of biological and personality features. Both nature and nurture shape individuals in a wide array of combinations. Citing a supposed "natural law" that locks a person's spiritual identity into rigid, male-or-female categories defies how Nature (with a capital N) actually functions.

But human beings, whose personal gender identities do not neatly fit into a harsh male-female taxonomy, have lived in every culture known to us. Natural, sexual selection has seemed confident that the majority of humans will choose other-sex partners with whom to mate so as to continue the species. But the natural world's chaotic thoughtfulness clearly allows for same-sex selection separate from the biological shape of reproduction. In this regard, Nature's laws seem far more patient of genuinely diverse

---

42. Patterson provides a useful investigation into the appearance of "there is no male and female" in Galatians 3:28a. For our purposes, it is pertinent to point out how disused this particular baptismal affirmation became in Christian history (*Forgotten Creed*, 121–53).

sexual endowments than most societies have been comfortable accommodating. And, if this is the case, these "laws" must be factored into any adequate definition of how we need to pursue justice regarding gender identity.[43]

Drilling down into these so-called laws of nature requires that we attend to another neglected area of growth in understanding, which I call *sexual justice*. Sexuality, or human bodiliness, underlies our earliest experience of self-sameness and personal wholeness. It also makes it possible for us to enact our desire for connection, for intimacy, and for communion with other persons. From a frankly spiritual perspective, we would be pretty incapable of desiring God without the mental and emotional abilities our bodies endow us with. In fact, we don't have to decide whether desire comes before sex, or if sex engenders desire, because we know that being embodied gives us the home for the inner selves we call our souls. But being embodied also requires that we negotiate the boundaries between ourselves and others. For every individual person's primal sexual energy reaches beyond for a sense of completion and wholeness from the earliest moments of life.

As a result, few areas of human activity have been as regulated as sexual activity. The significance of reproduction for the species and for societal life has birthed both laws and taboos in abundance. But the perceived need to regulate sexuality has also fostered man-made laws that prioritized power and order more than they cared for the rights or happiness of individual persons, particularly women. Religiously, law also became the prism through which to regard human sexuality in ways that inhibit an individual's freedom—with very mixed results. Fortunately, the balance between law and freedom has recently begun to shift—not everywhere, for sure—in the direction of an individual's access to sexual fulfillment. Legal frameworks imposed upon adult sexual activity in the name of morality have been too constrained, both

---

43. Walden recently wrote, "What the life stories of trans people show us is that we do not yet understand Scripture, that 'male and female He created them' is not a template, but a mystery, one deep enough that we cannot yet fully map its contours but must approach it with hearts humbled by love" ("Gender, Sex, and Other Nonsense," 26).

by attitudes about pure and impure body fluids as well as by ancient philosophical notions of the so-called "natural law" that I will shortly argue no longer constitutes the realm of the "natural."[44]

Bringing the perspective of justice to this issue can broaden the framework in which believing Christians might envision themselves as both sexual and spiritual persons.[45] Here, I will not take too deep a dive into the theory of natural law that Christianity inherited from pagan Stoic philosophers. Suffice it to say that it grew apace, by the Middle Ages, into a metaphysical system that attempted to articulate universal rational principals of moral action. It prized so-called rational activity, discovering what causes had which effects, and then judging some to be "natural" (right according to the nature of things) and others "unnatural" (wrong, though not necessarily morally imputable).

Yet, as carefully defined by Thomas Aquinas, natural law had a much more limited meaning than its later legalistic applications. It named our ability to reason about the truth of things in themselves, i.e., the world as it *really* is—not *ideally* as construed according to certain transcendent ideas.[46] Accordingly, reason alone contains few primary demands of this "law," e.g., do good and avoid evil. All others are secondary, or derived, based on implications that reason spelled out—normally by male, often clerical, academics or jurists.

But, too often, this meant that human *actions*, rather than human beings as free, moral actors, became the subject of this so-called natural, moral law. Human acts were deemed right or wrong based on how a so-called effect was determined by a specific kind of cause. For example, the action of swinging a hammer was moral if its effect drove a nail; immoral if it bashed in a skull. Because

---

44. Weil claims, "Christians have never said, so far as I am aware, *why* chastity (and more especially virginity) possesses a spiritual value. This is a serious lacuna, and one that keeps away a great many souls from Christ" (*Letter*, 43).

45. As the late author John O'Donohue puts it: "The body is the mirror where the secret world of the soul comes to expression. The body is a sacred threshold; and it deserves to be respected, minded, and understood in its spiritual nature" (*Anam Cara*, 47).

46. Dinter, *Beyond Naïve Belief*, 245–46.

human generation took place through the sexual intercourse of a male and a female, the procreative act was said to determine the most correct, if not the only, moral use of sexual arousal and enactment. The end determined the means, strictly and completely. In matters of sexuality, animals and humans shared the same bed: sex was what all animals, rational and otherwise, engaged in.

Sexual justice seeks to rebalance how believers can weigh the manifest good against the potential damage inherent in human sexuality, without loading the scale with predetermined "rational" ends. For, if we have learned anything through the expansion of reason and scientific knowledge, confining goodness in sexual relations to procreation constitutes an injustice foisted upon people for centuries. Responding justly today recognizes that law has too often been an instrument of repression. A long history of inequality imposed by males on females in sexual and social relationships has rightly been exposed as a moral evil.

Doing justice in matters of sexuality seeks to restore the *imago Dei* as male and female (Gal 3:28), no longer as binary opposites, but as a reconciled whole that allows for a range of individual expressions. For Christians, for whom the binary of male and female is subsumed in Christ, the firstborn of a new humanity, sexual characteristics amount to a relative statement of a person's unique identity. Our habit of absolutizing them has imprisoned people in unwanted roles, unequal treatment, and even forms of sexual slavery. If, instead, we relativize sexual differences, we can reimagine sexual expression as even more basic to human beings' pursuit of the good, the true, and the beautiful beyond its vital, but not exclusively procreative function.

At the same time, we can't ignore evolution's inbuilt competitive thrust, so often expressed through dominating sexual attitudes and behaviors. Calling out the supposed "survival of the fittest" as racist and sexist has helped us uncover deeper truths about how we evolved as a species. In reality, groups and societies practicing cooperation have been the real engine of growth and progress, not competitive victories.[47] We might even call this a version of the

---

47. Wilson traces the evolution of "eusociality" (true social condition)

This I Believe

"mystery that was kept secret for long ages, but now disclosed" (Rom 16:25-26). Cooperation that champions diversity, not treating difference or variety as a problem, makes for a heritage that humans should gratefully acknowledge.

Even more, sexual justice, as a practice, insists on naming and condemning every act by which sexual expression conceals power over another rather than respect, love, and affection. We continue to carry within our hormones and brains residues of the evolutionary dynamics known as sexual selection. Here, competition does play a role in how sexuality is enacted. Sex operates along a broad spectrum that easily lends itself to displays and actions—we call it lust—when the beauty inherent in sexual love descends into moral and physical ugliness.

A long record of men abusing women, employing rape or demanding sexual favors, haunts any effort to uphold the good, the true, and the beautiful of our gendered selves. Hence, uncovering, calling out, and prohibiting sexual abuse, both morally and legally, as a grave injustice constitutes a genuine imperative. At the same time, justice is not served by putting a fence around adult sexual activity, seeing it only moral and right when exercised in the confines of a marriage covenant. That covenant, seen from a perspective I will develop shortly as sacramental when lived in love and fidelity, has nevertheless fostered some repressive, unjust relations that subvert its sacredness.

For sexuality, and our ability to form just and loving relationships—whether characterized by *eros, philia,* or *agapē*[48]—lies deeper in the human psyche/soul than their inhabiting heterosexual marriage. If we would reweave adult sexuality into an integral, spiritual picture, we need to be honest about the ambivalence inherent in sexuality. That's a given. But we also must be willing to go

---

beginning with insects up through "group selection" that favors cooperation among its members: "Human beings are prone to be moral—do the right thing, hold back, give aid to others, sometimes at personal risk—because natural selection has favored those interactions of group members benefitting the group as a whole" (*Social Conquest,* 109, 247).

48. Generally understood as sexual love, friendship, and unconditional love.

the extra mile: to affirm the joy and the beauty in sexuality itself, despite its shadow side. The popularity of pornography, though often degrading and misanthropic, tells us something about people's need for access to an appreciative regard for sexuality and bodiliness, their own and that of idealized others. In fact, most people struggle with achieving a healthy body image that allows for mutuality and trust in sexual actions! But unless religious people see the justness in the case that much human joy is embedded here, in our being embodied souls, faith will always fail to prize a vital element of created beauty.

A final word: where does this leave sexual morality? It leaves it within the framework of moral and spiritual development by which we make a whole range of judgments of right or wrong, wise or foolish. Children need to be educated appropriately about their bodies and the bodies of others and to be assured their bodies belong to themselves and no one else. Adolescents need to be guided in recognizing the benefits and the risks inherent in their burgeoning sexual selves. The opposite, i.e., shaming young people about their sexuality, has done immeasurable harm. Young adults, whose prefrontal cortexes develop more slowly than their urges to copulate, should be taught the values of equality and responsibility in their sexual discoveries. Adults with full access to their sexuality should be free to gift themselves lovingly and unselfishly to others. For, without love and affection, the giver is a fraud and a user. Should that gifting occur within a committed marriage, individuals commit themselves not only to the beauty of self-giving, but to its ascesis or limitations as well. In the words of Leonard Cohen, who drew an almost monastic image of marriage:

> I think marriage is the hottest furnace of the spirit today. Much more difficult than solitude, much more challenging for people who want to work on themselves. It's a situation in which there are no alibis, excruciating most of the time . . . but it's only in this situation that any kind of work can be done.[49]

---

49. 1975 interview with Paul Williams (https://www.wisdompills.com/15-leonard-cohen-quotes-life-love-poetry).

This I Believe

Submitting ourselves to the judgment of Christ calls for searing honesty. But this honesty opens us to the depths of mercy and compassion that yield ways of life to be celebrated.

A last, but highly contentious, consideration raises the question of the meaning of *reproductive justice*. To some, this can only mean recognizing the absolute right of a fertilized ovum to be brought to birth. To others, this refers to the relative, but legally established, right of a woman to decide whether to bring a pregnancy to term. Briefly (and I write this at my peril), there is right on both sides of the question. Can we find a path out of the uncompromising conflict of views by recognizing some truth beyond the opposing claims?

Only if we admit that "rights" are never absolute, that justice requires us to reframe the moral and ethical issues involved. Contemporary physics, biology, and psychology have made convincing arguments that, at deeper levels of understanding of the natural world, our intuition alone easily misleads us. For their part, religious intuitions often function well on the affective level, providing comfort and coping mechanisms in crisis situations. But, like other intuitions, they often fall short of grasping the complex character of reality that makes even thoughtful judgments of "good" and "evil" inadequate to the matter.

That human life is present from the first moment of conception, and so is inviolable, ranks as this kind of intuition. It seeks to assign personhood, and the rights to "life, liberty, and the pursuit of happiness," to a fertilized egg, but one whose fate in the unfolding process of reproduction remains highly uncertain. Here, the brute facts of biology reveal the statistical uncertainty that the conceptus will reach maturity some months later. They also suggest strongly that what we call "personhood" emerges gradually yet uncertainly, through developing neural processes. While medical advances in prenatal rescues of fraught pregnancies have moved a fetus's viability outside the womb toward earlier stages, they will always be limited. Neither the existence of a fetal heartbeat nor the appearance of a primitive brain stem yet constitute an individual separate from the woman bearing this potential child.

Recognizing this developmental process argues against full personhood at the earliest stage of pregnancy. Writing from the perspective of Roman Catholic moral theology, I would raise the argument that mainstream moral theologians, from the eleventh-century Anselm of Canterbury, through the Catechism of the Council of Trent, St. Alphonsus Liguori in the seventeen hundreds, to the last-century moralist Cardinal Mercier, all held an earlier tradition on the process called "ensoulment." They explicitly denied that a human "soul" (hence, person) could possibly be present from the very beginning.

Yet Catholic sentiment began to shift away from this more traditional understanding of delayed personhood. The catalyst was not moral theology or reasoning, but an impulse to affirm the Blessed Virgin Mary's sinlessness. Burdened with Augustine's early medieval concept that all human beings were "stained" by original sin through sexual intercourse, some Catholic theologians felt it imperative to declare Mary the mother of Jesus exempt from it. They conceived of a teaching called the Immaculate Conception, which, as defined by Pope Pius IX, declared Mary sinless "from the first moment of her conception" (*in primo instanti suae conceptionis*)[50] preserving her free from all stain of original sin.

But, as we have been arguing throughout this lengthy essay, a "stain" attaching to one's soul is a metaphor. As I argued earlier, a metaphor, by definition, does not land or define a reality univocally, but contains a literal falsity as a condition of its having real truth value.[51] Seeking to preserve the affective role that devotion to Mary served in Catholic life, the definition literalized a state of holiness, or "sinlessness." It declared an inimitable moral condition to be the result of a biological event (Mary's sexual generation by her parents) and made it a putative condition that Catholics must necessarily believe for salvation!

At a perilous time in the history of Catholicism, this Marian doctrine played doctrinal offense in fortifying the Church's defense against Enlightenment rationalism. Hearkening back to the

---

50. Denzinger and Schönmetzer, eds., *Enchiridion*, 1641.
51. See above, n20.

veneration of the Virgin during the Middle Ages, this essentially Romantic-age intuition was then elevated to an identity marker for all Catholic believers. As the Church expanded demographically, spawned multiple religious orders, and sent missioners far and wide, Catholicism was developing a hyper-organizational and literalist mindset that collapsed any distinction between law and belief. The 1917 Code of Canon Law attempted to close that circle definitively. Accordingly, belief in God's creation of an individual soul at the moment that couples fertilely copulated embedded itself in the common Catholic imagination. Any notion that nature operated more randomly, and proceeded more organically, ran up against an ideological boundary. It asserted that, before fertilization, no ensouled person existed. After the sperm entered the egg, a new immortal soul existed for all eternity.

By way of summary, it appears to me that the dogmatic definition resembles the ancient rabbinical practice of erecting a "fence around the Torah." In principle, one never could violate the commandment (for instance) against "boiling a young goat in its mother's milk" (Exod 34:26) if you never ate meat and dairy in the same meal. The example may be extreme, but in both cases the intention is similar. The rabbis sought to protect the Law from violation while Pius IX saw himself protecting the Church's devotion to the Mother of God. Both stem from deep religious intuitions, but neither represents the heart of the matter for a majority of observant Jews or even for many believing Catholics.

The lens of reproductive justice seeks to balance two so-called "rights": one that a human conceptus may be endowed with and a second that an individual woman should be free to exercise. That is, the freedom to decide, in the early stages of a pregnancy, whether to carry the developing fetus to birth. We seem to have failed to articulate principles of just decision-making in situations where these claims might conflict.[52] Absolutizing two opposing

---

52. Shields, a close observer of abortion politics, citing research that most abortion providers "usually dislike providing abortions at some point in the second trimester when the fetus becomes more recognizably human," calls for a compromise: "one that grants broad access to abortion in the first trimester but largely restricts it in the second and third." He suggests that both justice

positions—a "right to life" vs. a "right to choose"—has shut down efforts to delegalize and depoliticize the question. From a religious perspective on justice, there will certainly be times when an unplanned pregnancy imposes a heavy burden on a woman, with or without a partner. In such a case, should she consciously "go the extra mile" and freely decide to accept the life developing inside of her, she accepts it as a gift of the Creator.

Should a woman be unable or unwilling to carry the pregnancy to term, she can *in justice* make a conscientious decision to terminate the pregnancy. But preventing women from making such a decision, particularly by politicized legal maneuvers, falls outside the ken of justice. Making even early termination illegal in the name of a moral imperative represents an unjust imposition of a highly dubious intuition unsupported by how nature itself works. Even more, the recent laws that have sought to outlaw *all* abortions, no matter a pregnant woman's circumstances, have deprived women of moral agency, nullified their autonomy, and made them subject to the will of a hyper-political minority. Resorting to coercive law sidesteps questions of justice *tout court*.

I believe in the Holy Spirit . . .

"Spirit," too, as a metaphor associates a physical force shared by all the living with the deepest spiritual bond both within God and with the created world.

What is called the *doctrine of the Holy Spirit* took some time to be formulated among early Christian communities. While wrenching controversies about the person of Christ, of his nature and divinity, were dividing the church into rigid orthodoxies, belief in the Spirit

---

and Americans' moral intuitions "will exert a moderating influence on abortion politics and incline us to balance clashing liberal claims" put forth by both the pro-choice and pro-life movements. ("Hard but Real Compromise," https://www.nytimes.com/2021/10/19/opinion/abortion-pro-life-movement.html.)

worked its way into the Creed quietly. As "the breath of God" that birthed the world and commissioned God's servants the prophets, this breath/spirit/wind (*pneuma*) crops up in the New Testament writings variously. As the practices in Hinduism and Buddhism have always captured, our very breath ties us to one another and to the world around us. Hence, the *rūach elohim* ("breath of God/mighty wind" in Genesis 1:1) is nothing other than the "breath of life." The early English physiologist William Harvey framed it this way: "There is nothing living that does not breathe, nor anything breathing that does not live." [53]

But, again, as a metaphor, the "Spirit" is no thing. It associates as deep a spiritual experience as we can name with a physical force that permeates the world we live in. Its portrayal as a dove descending at Jesus' baptism began as another metaphor that got literalized. Luke alone adds "in bodily form." But the image refers mainly to the action of "descending [from heaven] like a dove" more than to the appearance of a specific winged creature. Luke also adds the ascription "Holy" (here and in Gabriel's announcement to Mary), which declares this Spirit a divine presence. "Holiness," based upon the temple vision of God's "otherness" in Isaiah 6 (*kadōsh, kadōsh, kadōsh*), speaks of the extreme degree of God's transcendence. As a modifier, "holy" prevents us from domesticating the divine, the mystery that we, too often, reshape in our own image, in our own likeness.

In Paul's writings, the Spirit breathes life into Christ's body, the church. In Mark (and Matthew), it is the power that anointed Jesus, but then drove him into the wilderness to confront the mythic Adversary. As above, Luke proposed that the same breath of God that moved over the waters in Genesis 1 engendered Mary's virgin pregnancy. In the Fourth Gospel, the Spirit continues Christ's own presence as the gift of forgiving sin and as the Advocate who makes manifest the union of Father and Son with the community of believers. This union in love defines God (Creator, Redeemer, Life-Giver) as the binding force of all that was, is, and will be.

---

53. Quoted in Jarvis, "What Happens When You Breathe," 66.

Extending the Narrative

The doctrine of the Triune God emerged, then, in and through the lived experience of communities of faith. Through hearing and retelling the story, and knowing Christ to be a real presence among them, they understood themselves as being given life by the Creator, graced by the Word, and reborn in the Spirit. Life and prayer in the Spirit preceded the doctrine; the experience of Christ alive gave rise to seeing the Holy Spirit as one with the Father and the Son.

But let's be clear that "Trinity," (or "three-ness") does not primarily function as a noun. It describes actions: life-giving movement, self-giving love, the fulfilling of all desire, and the communion of all things with their Source and End. The One in whom "we live and move and have our being" (Acts 17:28) enacts oneness in diversity and unifies the past with the present and both with the future within and through us and all created things. Poured out on all living things, it also crafts a "call and response" with creation whose echo engenders the people we call the church.[54]

The holy catholic church . . .

As a sacrament or sign of universal solidarity and of the intimacy that human creatures share with the divine, the church needs to practice blessing in its worship and life to enable her to do the work of reconciliation.

What follows in the Creed—*"the holy catholic church"*—flows from this lived experience: an *ekklesia*, a community called together in the image of the people of Israel. But this people is now assembled from "all the nations" as the prophets of Israel looked for. The adjective "catholic" in the Creed means universal or all-embracing. When capitalized, it can refer to the largest ecclesial group of

---

54. Richard Rohr's cosmic, yet everyday, mysticism is summed up as, "*All that you have ever seen with your eyes is the self-emptying of God into multitudinous physical and visible forms*" (*Divine Dance*, 126). I can't think of a better way to introduce this particular historic form that we term "the church."

This I Believe

Christians (the *Roman* Catholic Church), but the small "c" contains the original meaning; hence it appears in the prayer books of other Christian communities.

Today, the word "church" triggers images of large organizations, many hierarchically organized, ensconced in basilicas, cathedrals, office buildings, parishes, etc. But the "catholic church" began as a radical effort to gather people from "every race and tongue, people, and nation" and proclaim their mutual solidarity as human creatures in the image and likeness of God. My eyes were opened to this notion when it was captured in the very first sentence of the Second Vatican Council's Pastoral Constitution on the Church in the Modern World: "The joys and the hopes, the griefs and anxieties of the [people] of this age, especially those who are poor or in any way afflicted, these too are the joys and the hopes, the griefs and anxieties of the followers of Christ."[55] Any less encompassing use of the word "church" reduces it to a cult among cults and demeans its very reason for being.

In fact, the same council had earlier declared that the church exists as a "sacrament" or a sign and symbol of a unified humanity.[56] In brief, the church is meant to be a beacon and an example for the whole of humanity, making manifest our common origin and end. At peace with itself and with the whole of creation, this image of humanity is nothing less than (in the aspirational symbolism of the book of Revelation) "the holy city" where God dwells immediately, in actuality and *religionlessly*. In a sense, the church only exists to make itself redundant. As St. Paul expressed it, then, we will no longer see "through a glass darkly" but know God intimately even as we are known by God, whose love remains the greatest gift the Spirit bestows (1 Cor 13:12).

We needn't waste too much ink on detailing the historical failures of the church, in all its expressions, to live up to this pacific, catholic, and humanitarian vision. As a contingent historical entity, the church in its many incarnations has suffered in diverse, often self-inflicted, ways. But, more importantly, it has sinned

---

55. *Documents of Vatican II, Gaudium et Spes*, 1, 198–99.
56. *Documents of Vatican II, Lumen Gentium*, 1, 15.

mightily, causing enormous suffering, harm, and even blessing murder. The sick legacy of its anti-Judaism, heretic hunting, inquisitional injustice, monarchical tyranny, anti-sexuality, gynophobic violence, and institutional arrogance could fill volumes. Whenever the catholicity of any Christian body descends into tribalism, nationalism, or partisan hatred, it surrenders any claim to share in *the* body of Christ. But admitting these tragedies and apostacies will only strengthen the paradox residing in the church's continued relevance.

Instead, I want to try and capture the essence of the *sacramentality* of the church as a reason for its endurance (despite itself) and for its promise in the twenty-first century. But first to clarify: when the Latin *sacramentum* became the West's term for the New Testament term *mystērion*, its meaning shrank. Previously, "mystery" had signaled more than a puzzle, cosmic or otherwise, now made clear. Rather, it proclaimed the newly unveiled depth of the divine/human intimacy at the heart of revelation itself.

Yet as a metaphor of this unseen reality, even the term "sacrament" still does not designate any *thing*, or entity, in itself. It seeks to catch the sense that Christ himself, the church, and all created things uncover or reveal more than themselves. Here is the paradox in this aspect of the Creed: As signs, sacraments reveal; but they always contain an element of concealment or unrevelation.[57] That is, Christ's humanity is the sacrament that conceals divinity at the same time that it reveals God's presence in historical time. For its part, the church reveals itself to be the locus of our communion with the divine, even as its sinfulness conceals its ultimate nature. As sacramental, all creatures, from microbes to planets, from quarks to galaxies, "tell the glory of God" even as they participate in the drama of evolutionary death and subsequent life.

This deeper reality, that all is sacred and participates in an unfolding union of Creator and created, tends to be lost or

---

57. Ker quoting Newman's early *Essays Critical and Historical*: "Revelation . . . is not a revealed *system*, but consists of a number of detached and incomplete truths belonging to a vast system unrevealed, of doctrines and injunctions mysteriously connected together . . ." (*Newman*, 122).

This I Believe

overwhelmed when dogmatic questions like "How many sacraments are there?" hold the floor. Dogmatic disputes aside, it is helpful to remember that St. Augustine called the special rituals of baptismal washing, anointing, and eucharistic celebrations "visible words." As such, the actions themselves, anchored in daily, physical realities, "say" or name something beyond them. The material elements employed in these actions—water, oil, bread, and wine—all signify a relationship only hinted at in their ritual use. But as visible and enacted signs, they declare the mystery of unitive love to be materially real in this time and in this place, and in the person receiving them. Hence, Augustine, among others, claimed that they imparted a "character," a very stamp annealed deep in a person's very being (or "soul" if you wish).

So sacramentality itself cannot be walled in by canons and laws. Not if what Gerard Manley Hopkins captured holds any truth: "The world is charged with the grandeur of God. / It will flame out, like shining from shook foil; / It gathers to a greatness, like the ooze of oil / Crushed."[58] Grasping this allows us to avoid arguments about valid or legal sacraments (let alone their number) even when we admit that communities will always seek to regulate their rituals. But if these rituals, in all their variety, express unselfish acts of love (*agapē*), then they have "validity" and participate in this mystery as St. Paul's famous hymn, confession, and vision in 1 Corinthians 13, cited above, eloquently expresses it.

At the same time, any adequate understanding of sacramental love and self-giving remains centered in the Christian Eucharist. So examining the term "Eucharist" will help to flesh out the rationale for the church itself according to the Creed. But, as importantly, it will help to articulate the church's need to be fully engaged in the work of justice, specifically the ministry of reconciliation. For, while the word "Eucharist" itself carries a lot of ambiguity, understanding its underlying meaning will free us from unhappy, even morbid, misconceptions.

Below, I will endeavor to undo some that resulted from over-literalizing the ancient roots of worship itself. For it has become

---

58. Hopkins, *Poems*, 15–16.

clear today that what Christians mean by liturgy or worship carries a stigma. Many millennials (and younger cohorts as well), even those whose parents grew up in the church, suffer a profound alienation from what the church stands for, how it realizes itself, and what gives it overall meaning or relevance. I hope that bringing some clarity to *eucharistia* as an action and a way-of-living might begin to rehabilitate what "giving praise and thanks to God" actually entails.

For Eucharist primarily denotes an effective act of blessing and thanksgiving before it ever refers to an object, even a sacred one. It denotes a surrender of control and an opening of the self to receiving a gift, even the gift of life itself. Anthropologically, it is rooted in early sacrificial practice but develops beyond it. Almost all ancient people "offered" sacrifice by setting aside (i.e., "making holy" or consecrating) material elements of life.

In many cases, offering sacrifice involved acts of violence that rendered the "offering" or (if an animal) the "victim" partially or wholly a gift to a deity. The sacrificial act encompassed surrender as well as gratitude. Literally that's what a "sacrifice" sought to accomplish: to express freedom from selfish concerns and gratefulness for gifts received. But, contrary to some catechetical explanations, the Eucharist only *arose from* these ancient roots; it is *not* a literal sacrifice. More deeply, it engages in an act of blessing and thanksgiving as a sacramental, but metaphorical, sacrifice. Any strength or virtue that it continues to have, as celebrated in Roman Catholic, Orthodox, or Reformation traditions, depends on this vital distinction.

Scripture and tradition attest that Jesus engaged in a eucharistic action at the Last Supper "on the night before he died." Giving a blessing over the bread and cup survives in Jewish prayer practice to the present day. But, in that setting, Jesus employed it to transform the meaning and the finality of his execution. Refusing his fate as a victim of political and religious violence, he offered a blessing before giving his body and blood in symbol as a gift to be shared. He commanded that his followers enact this blessing, breaking, and sharing the bread/body and wine/blood "in remembrance of me." The command originally had nothing to do with offering anything but a powerful act of blessing, thanksgiving, and remembering the gift he made of his life for others. Jesus consecrated, made sacred and holy, his self-giving, transforming his death on the cross from meaningless tragedy to renewable gift secured by his life-in-God beyond death. When we obey his command to "do this in remembrance of me," that is bless God, take and eat, take and drink, he becomes more than a memory, but an actual presence.

The earliest sources we have for Christian worship recount and recite the blessing that gave its name (*eucharistia*) to the gifts received in communion. They make no mention of offering sacrifice—even noting that God the Giver does not require them (echoing Psalm 50:12–14).[59] But, over time, Christians felt the need to claim that *they*, and not their Jewish contemporaries, were the legitimate heirs of the worship in the temple. In the place of understanding Jesus' "obediently accepting death . . . even death upon the cross" as a heroic act of love for his friends, his death on the cross was increasingly viewed through the lens of "offering a [ritual] sacrifice." In these polemical circumstances, worship "in spirit and in truth" (John 4:23) seemed a weak and uncertain alternative to the age-old practice of sacrificial death. The consequences for the church's mission and role in society have been fateful.

At the same time, we have to admit that several powerful scriptural passages too easily favor an understanding of Jesus' death in overtly literal, sacrificial terms. But I am contending that, after some literary sleuthing, all these allusions to sacrifice carry more meaning as strong metaphors. As I have argued throughout this journey through the Christian story, metaphor and symbol generate more fruitful beliefs than do stale literal readings of events or persons in the narrative. In fact, when "sacrifice" is used in the New Testament writings, it appears in several, very different and, I am arguing, nonliteral contexts: in Paul, for moral exhortation as

---

59. "If I were hungry, I would not tell you, / for the world and all that it in it is mine. / Do I eat the flesh of bulls, / or drink the blood of goats? / Offer to God a sacrifice of thanksgiving, / and pay your vows to the Most High." The denunciation of animal sacrifice is even more explicit in Isaiah 66:3–4.

Extending the Narrative

he champions faith in place of fulfilling legal requirements; in the Fourth Gospel, for emphasizing how Jesus did *not* die a victim, but laid down his life for his friends; in the Letter to the Hebrews, for reimagining the very concept of worship; and in Revelation, for bolstering persecuted believers for whom the "slain" Lamb is none other than the living Lion of the tribe of Judah.

In Appendix A, I offer a more technical examination of the texts just referenced, which undergirds my argument that "sacrifice" and the "priesthood" appear in them as metaphors. The terms have to be understood as ready references from the imaginative world of earliest Christianity before its schism from its Jewish matrix. They only allude to what actual *cōhanim* (priests) did when they burnt incense, grain, or animal parts on an altar in Herod's Temple in Jerusalem. These authors use familiar religious terms. But they all press them into the service of opening a formerly unimagined horizon of grace and forgiveness. In the "new age" seen to be dawning, *eucharistia* replaced the old order.

Evidence for this alternative view of worship actually survived in the fourth-century Roman canon or eucharistic prayer. It professed explicitly that the church is offering a "sacrifice of praise," not a literal one, but a metaphorical and sacramental one. This "new covenant" eucharistic meal, with its blessing, sharing, and receiving gifts, replaced the literal sacrifices offered in temple worship. But as the first-millennium church distanced itself from its Jewish heritage, it also took on many of the forms of imperial Roman society, both in the East and the West. As of old, priests alone offered sacrifice, shifting leadership in the church from "overseers" to bishops, "elders" to priests, and "servants" to deacons, a burgeoning hierarchy managing the "dioceses" of the Roman Empire. In place of offering "a sacrifice of praise," the *sacramental* presence of Jesus' Passover from death to life was said to be made real again, not through the renewed gift of the Spirit, but through the totemic recital of the "words of consecration" by an ordained *hierus* or *sacerdotus*, a priest such as slaughtered animals in temples in Rome or in Jerusalem. Once the literal application of the idea of sacrifice began to dominate, it spawned a twisted effort to explain how eucharistic worship filled the bill as a superior ritual sacrifice.

This I Believe

But neither the adopting of the lens of sacrifice, nor the trappings of sacral priesthood, were divinely ordained or necessary for the truth of the gospel to be lived or celebrated. They were the contingent effects of historical personalities and forces. No, Constantine did not conquer another army in Christ's name; that's propaganda. Then, the unbaptized emperor took advantage of the growth of Christian belief among both educated and illiterate citizens of the empire to legitimate himself. His favoring Christianity over other religions presaged what many politicians before and since have done. His "sacral kingship" (later inherited by the pope) required that power be wielded univocally in a "for us" or "against us" manner. This division led inexorably to setting off one group against another: orthodox against heretics, believers against nonbelievers, Christians against Jews, men over against women, etc.

The churches of the Reformation rejected what had become the doctrine of transubstantiation of the bread and wine by the power of an ordained priest. Out went the "sacrifice of the Mass" as well. To counter these denials, Catholicism doubled down at the Council of Trent (1545 to 1563). In doing so, it froze eucharistic worship and clung to the need for priests to offer sacrifice, albeit an "unbloody" one. But none of the scriptural sources for Jesus' sacrifice support this strange combination.

So once we admit this simple truth, it makes my argument firmer: both sacrifice and priesthood have metaphorical, not literal, value today in the real world. Their truth value arises from the way they deny any literal truth claim they might possess. For in reality, Jesus was *not* a high priest nor was he sacrificed. As I argued above, these literal truths supply the metaphors with their affective power and their truth value for believers. By first resisting applying both "priest" and "sacrifice" to Jesus on the literal, historical level, we unearth what the author of Hebrews called "fitting" (2:10) on the metaphorical, referential, and symbolic level. The quixotic nature of these affirmations illustrates a key point in this study: paradox, operating through plentiful metaphors, has more potential for expressing what is real in the realm of faith. Not because paradox celebrates the irrational. But because paradox, often seen as the "coincidence of opposites," frees us from the dead end of literalism, and the religious ideology and intolerance it spawns. Via paradox, we are closer to capturing what the Gospels so desperately seek to convey about sin and forgiveness. As Paul expressed the paradox of the cross: "God's foolishness outwits human wisdom" (1 Cor 1:25).

As I understand it, the failure of preachers and teachers to grasp the deeply poetic and symbolic images and language of the New Testament has left people stranded in Flatland, a binary, two-dimensional world of either fact or fiction.[60] Christian faith became one version or other of a deal about obedience by which believers won or lost the favor of God. The different consequences for believers were stark, a sad place for the "good news" to lodge itself in the minds of believers.

But I believe we can change a lot of popular misconceptions about who Christians are and what they believe if we recalibrate our sense of worship itself. For what is real as well as sacramental is the *eucharistic action* itself. In it, we give praise and thanks to the one Jesus called *Abba* for the gifts of life, creation, of calling Israel, of sending the Son who bore the cross, but was raised up to send the Spirit upon the bread and wine of the church's gathering. Within this thanksgiving, we especially bless God by remembering the words over the bread and cup by which Jesus continues to offer the church his very life. Even when Christian worship does not include any form of communion service, the actions of proclaiming the word, preaching, and offering praise in song themselves function sacramentally. They are signs of Christ's presence in the word and the Spirit's power to move believers to "Make a joyful noise to the LORD . . . break forth into joyous song and sing praises" (Ps 98:4).

---

60. Borg cites Edwin A. Abbott's 1884 *Flatland*: "Flatland is a two-dimensional universe having only length and width (and thus lacking height and depth), a plane inhabited by two-dimensional creatures—squares, triangles, rectangles, and so forth." Borg sees this as "an image for the modern worldview" that excludes experiences that "suggest that reality is far more mysterious than any and all of our domestications—whether scientific or religious—make it out to be" (*God We Never Knew*, 45).

This I Believe

Christians have rarely attended to an important analogy to the end of ritual sacrifice found in rabbinic Judaism. After the temple's destruction, the early rabbis sacramentalized their *talmūd Tōrāh*, i.e., "study of the Law" and its full implications replaced literal sacrifice as the way that Israel would continue to fulfill its covenant with God. The temple gave way to the *bet ha midrash*, the synagogue, the place where God's presence (*shekinah*) now dwelled. For its part, the *ekklēsia*, the body of Christ and the temple of the Spirit, where the word is spoken and the bread is broken, plays a like role "until he comes again." It represents the "worship in spirit and truth" that replaced any fixed locale of worship ("neither on this mountain nor in Jerusalem," John 4:21) offered by a fixed hieratic official.

In these terms, the Eucharist remains revolutionary in its claims that Christ's death and exaltation (metaphorically his "entrance into the Holy of Holies") replaced bloody sacrificial worship as had been practiced by Jews and Gentile pagans for centuries. Instead, the literal understanding of being "redeemed by the blood of Jesus" turned his self-offering, his martyr's death, into a gruesome transaction, not a gracious gift. It also began a long process by which the spilling of the "blood of the martyrs" could be harnessed as a rationale for shedding others' blood: of heretics, of Jews, and of so-called infidels. The rest is our tragic history.

The belief statement that I am offering here derives from my studying and celebrating this central sacrament that so defines the Creed's "the catholic church" from *both* sides of the altar: minister of and ministered to. In my understanding, the "words of consecration" must lose their almost shamanic power, uniquely wielded by a so-called priest alone. They recede into a ritual remembering (*anamnēsis*) that itself occasions how the gift of the Spirit of Jesus' risen life is renewed in the sacrament. Believers participate not as suppliants, but as partners or companions who receive the gifts of the altar, not as bread and wine, but as the gift of Christ's life-beyond-death. Eucharist results in communion shared through Christ in God's own life of love outpoured in the Holy Spirit.

In sum, the sacramentality of the church is best expressed when it adopts and propagates a eucharistic mode of life and worship. For knowing how to give thanks, learning the practice of gratitude, sits squarely in the center of "the good life."[61] It inculcates compassion, opens hearts and minds to forgiveness and reconciliation, and frees one from the self-absorption that allows us to do the work of justice in the world. If the kingdom ever is to come, it will be because we have adopted lively thanksgiving and learned to share the gifts that none of us deserve, but that each and all of us have inherited. That heritage and its future call the church to be more than it may ever appear to be: a communion of "God's beloved ... who are called to be saints" (Rom 1:7).

The communion of saints . . .

The idea of church expands into a radically communitarian view of humanity beyond any historical or present-day organization, local or global.

When the Creed next professes "the communion of saints," it is affirming that the bonds of love and mutual affection of all believers are themselves sacramental, i.e., signs of the mystery of our share in the divine Communion. But this article of faith deepens these bonds beyond the confines of any one generation's membership in the body. This belief arises from Jesus' own interpretation of the message to Moses: "I am the God of Abraham, Isaac and Jacob ... all are alive in him" (Luke 20:7–8); from Paul's confidence in Christ's return as judge of both the living and the dead; and from the Letter to the Hebrews' naming the "great cloud of witnesses" who surround persecuted believers and strengthen them. The

---

61. Kimmerer writes, "What would it be like to be raised on gratitude, to speak to the natural world as a member of a democracy of species, to raise a pledge of *inter*dependence?" (*Braiding Sweetgrass* 112). "Cultures of gratitude must also be cultures of reciprocity. Each person, human or no, is bound to every other in a reciprocal relationship" (115).

communion of saints expands the idea of the church to include all those alive in Christ beyond any historical or present-day organization, local or global.

Beginning in the last century, ancestry research, the popular activity of "finding your roots," has grown exponentially. But long before ancestral records were stored "in the cloud," Judaism prized its ethnic and religious sense of oneness with Abraham and Sarah and their progeny in Isaac. Christianity developed from this ethos a spiritual and moral sense that bound together the generations of believers, first through appropriating Abraham's paternity of all the nations, then via its reverence for the early martyrs, and in its lively remembrance of those who began to be popularly known as "the saints."

For Paul, "saint" named every Christian believer, but historical disputes about holiness tended to narrow the term to exceptional men and women. Over time, this eventually developed into "the cult of the saints," which fostered remembrance and intercessory prayers addressed to the "affirmed ancestors" (Heb 11:2). The practice continues to be a central feature in Catholic devotional and prayer life. At the same time, such devotion can often reduce what Vatican II called "the universal call to holiness"[62] to those who canonically qualified to bear the official title. Happily, recent practices have expanded the litany of the saints to include other witnesses to faith, hope, love, and justice, as well as loved ones "who have lived faithfully a hidden life and rest in unvisited tombs."[63]

How, then, do we understand the notion of the intercession of the Blessed Virgin and the saints that has anchored so much piety over the ages? Certainly not by seeing them as some kind of holy or wholly alien others. Believers are joined with them, their memory, and their impact within the bond of communion we share in and through the Spirit who "intercedes for the saints according to the will of God" (Rom 8:27). The saints who went before us cannot be said to act like the "heavenly council" whom

---

62. *Documents of Vatican II, Gaudium et Spes*, 39.
63. Eliot, *Middlemarch*, 898.

God Almighty consults for advice, striking bargains or putting in pleas for their clients.[64] We have one Advocate, the Spirit that dwells within us and in whom we have communion with the saints, living and deceased. Surely, we can understand that much of the medieval piety that monetized prayers to the saints, and which the Protestant Reformation rejected, actually distanced us from the saints who became "other" and unlike us. Popular culture (and some ecclesiastical needs for approval) will always valorize individuals such as Theresa of Calcutta. But setting her above sincere, practicing believers only puts putative "sanctity" out of reach instead of calling people into a deeper grasp that they are "partners in a heavenly calling" (Heb 3:1).

When we pray, we are recognizing our mutual dependence on the mystery of grace that has been given us. Asking the Blessed Virgin, Saints Peter and Paul, Francis and Claire, the martyrs and uncounted others for "favors" resembles a transaction, not an act of faith. In popular devotion, they can too easily resemble the superheroes that have such a powerful hold on imaginations of both my grandsons and more mature folk. Still, as part of that "great cloud of witnesses" (Heb 12:1) they are joined to us, not as separate individuals but as some of the millions of others taken up into Christ and living through their communion with us. Praying for the poor, the sick, our family, for peace, for healing—all these actions deepen our solidarity with and in the communion of saints.

When I recently taught college classes, I had the students read Rabbi Harold S. Kushner's *When Bad Things Happen to Good People*. In this book, which has never been out of print in forty years, he makes several salient points about prayer that have validity in a Christian context. Prayer, he affirms, redeems us from the isolation and the solipsism that too easily leads people to despair. It does this by creating a sense of communion. We do not pray to change fate or other people, but rather to change ourselves. He

---

64. This ancient mythic conception of how divinity interacts with the world, reflected in the very opening of Genesis (1:26: "Let us make humankind in our image . . ."), forms the background to Micaiah ben Imlah's "lying spirit" (1 Kgs 22:15–23). See also Jer 22:18–22, Job 1:6–2, Phil 2:5–11, and Heb 1:5–14.

advocates that people pray as did Jacob as he prepared for what he feared would be Esau's wrath (Gen 32:9–12). As the rabbi observes, "people who pray for strength, hope, and courage so often find resources of strength, hope, and courage that they did not have before they prayed."[65]

Rather than petitioning for favors, he advocates prayers of blessing and thanksgiving that open the person who is praying to wholeness in the midst of our brokenness. In such self-forgetting prayer, we can find some intimations of transcendence even in the contradictions we experience. These prayers can help us rediscover that creation itself possesses a deep underlying goodness uncanceled by the evils that threaten to overwhelm us. In this way, one never prays alone, but always joins in both a silent and sung chorus of praise, a communion with the living and all those who have gone before us.

Sadly, persons in other cultures who reverenced their ancestors in different ways than Europeans did were, until recently, labeled ancestor worshippers or pagans. But these practices of honoring ancestors stem from living persons' high regard for those who bequeathed them their history, culture, and DNA. They exist on a spectrum with the Creed's insistence that all the living and dead make up the fabric of the new creation. Far from being an assertion that "outside the church there is no salvation," the communion of the saints attests to a quintessential human desire to be connected across lifetimes in acts of real *communion* that unite generations across time as well as join together members of otherwise diverse societies and races. Its religious meaning is firmly anchored in our biology, social bonding, and cultural life.

Beyond this, the communion of saints as an article of faith sees our biological bonds with the living and the dead as inherently spiritual and of great value. Professing it also commits the believer to a radically communitarian view of humanity. As such, it reveals that individualism, as currently touted in consumerist societies, fails the test of human solidarity. It shows itself to be shallow and self-serving. Beyond that, this bond of communion

---

65. Kushner, *When Bad Things*, 141.

recognizes our real, sacramental union with the created world and our obligation to protect its health and integrity for generations to come. Cut off from this deeper understanding of communion, the church becomes just another tribe exploiting the natural world, alienated from brother sun, sister moon, mother earth, the gifts of nature, and the mortality that makes us human rather than cyborgs.[66] Lastly, the communion of saints grounds salvation in the here and now of our mutual bonds of love. Without these, "heaven" only represents an escape, not a flowering of God's own Spirit within the human community.

The forgiveness of sins . . .

The church is commissioned by the Spirit to carry out the ministry of gratuitous forgiveness and reconciliation as the very reason for its existence.

When the Creed follows with "the forgiveness of sins," it enacts our bond of communion with the divine Mystery in a radical, yet practical, fashion. Why does this article appear here in the Creed? The forgiveness of sins, what Paul in 2 Corinthians refers to as "the ministry of reconciliation," lies at the heart of what Christ's church, his body, exists in time to bring about. It follows upon and stems from the church's realizing itself in time through the ministry of word and sacrament. In all the Gospels, this work occupies the center of Jesus' own ministry. It might even be said that Christ rises to "inspire" the disciples when he breathes the Spirit on them

---

66. The all-encompassing, or cosmic-humanist, vision of Francis of Assisi continues to be celebrated in his "Canticle of the Creatures," which expresses blessing and praise for our brothers Sun, Wind, and Fire and our sisters Moon, Water, Mother Earth and, finally, Bodily Death "from whom no one can escape." Beginning with the words *Laudato si'*, "the first poem written in the emerging Italian vernacular," it poetically underscores the communion we share with the natural world in both our living and our dying. It provides the main theme of the previously cited 2015 encyclical letter of Pope Francis *Laudato Si'*. Find the original text and context in Cahill, *Mysteries*, 168–70.

that they might forgive sins (the Fourth Gospel) or sends the Spirit in tongues of fire on Pentecost (Acts of the Apostles) to empower them to preach repentance and forgiveness.

These post-resurrection commissions echo Jesus' own teaching in the Sermon on the Mount about the "surpassing justice" (Matt 5:20) that he urges on his followers. As regards forgiveness and reconciliation, disciples are directed to take the initiative, even in situations where someone has a complaint against them, and "leave their gifts at the altar" (i.e., interrupt an act of worship) and first go be reconciled. Reconciliation with a brother or sister, in this instance, "surpasses" a typical act of sacrifice. As Jesus later says, echoing the prophet Hosea, "I desire mercy, not sacrifice" (Matt 9:13).

When Paul takes up a description of this ministry, he, too, moves in an unlikely direction. In his struggle to defend his ministry, the impetus behind 2 Corinthians, the apostle presents Jesus' death *on analogy with* propitiatory sacrifice, i.e., one that made up for sin. But it is not, as would become enshrined in St. Anselm's theology of atonement, required of a "God-man." Rather, God responded to Jesus' martyr's death, not by punishing any party for its sinful injustice, but by absolving "their sins" in an act of reconciling justice (2 Cor 5:19).[67]

Expanding on the very concept of "justice," Paul insists on this divine paradox: the death of Jesus, the just one, did not draw God's condemnation. Rather it revealed the depth of divine mercy. God showed love for "sinners" in the very situation where a more miserly (and worldly) notion of justice would require payback. God's reconciling with self-alienated humanity is activated in an undeserved act of pure grace. The template is then set: Jesus' followers are to act accordingly and forgive sins. But not because the sinners deserve it. Rather, forgiveness challenges both, as the

---

67. The tragic consequences that flowed from Matthew 22:25 ("Then the people as a whole answered, 'His blood be on us and on our children!'") became universalized into the "teaching of contempt" and its baleful consequences cannot be overstated. Gale notes, "Matthew's first readers likely related the verse to the Jerusalem population, devastated in 70 CE" ("Matthew," *Jewish Annotated New Testament*, 52).

disciple becomes more closely united to Christ and the other is freed from the power of sin. Forgiveness, freely given, has greater power to reach out, humanize, and rehabilitate a miscreant than a moral or judicial system intent on punishment alone.

Believing in the forgiveness of sins requires a leap of faith, one that recaptures the divine judgment of creation in Genesis: that it was "very good." If the church carries out the mission of forgiveness, she reenacts God's loving satisfaction with all created things and participates in God's "justifying" or saving the world from its own self-destructive energies. All this comports with the hundreds of times that the words "forgive" and "forgiveness" appear in the New Testament.

But when church authorities introduced harsh penitential discipline, they impoverished the grace by which we share in God's justice, reducing being "just" or blameless to an individual's moral status. Further, in Catholicism, they later restricted forgiveness to the administration of a priest, once again confusing grace with power, a gift for a reward only granted to those formally penitent. But the task of forgiveness is entrusted to the whole church and the ministry of reconciliation occurs in broader settings than "sacramental confession." Feeding the hungry, clothing the naked, visiting prisoners, and healing the sick are all graced actions prompted by the Spirit, the free giving of love irrespective of anyone's "just deserts." These so-called charitable deeds make real the free acts of forgiveness that best imitate God's justice-making love, in sending the Son and the Spirit to reconcile the world to Godself.

In reality, the church ritually celebrates and receives the gift of reconciliation, not mainly in the extraordinary setting of auricular confession, but in every celebration of the Eucharist. We bring ourselves, together with all our individual and communal faults and sins, so as to be forgiven and renewed, to be refreshed and fed, to open ourselves to the outpouring of the Spirit of Christ's resurrection. Having received this gift, freely given and renewed, worshippers are sent back to their daily lives (in the old word's *Ite, missa est*) as agents of reconciliation. For Catholics, "going to Mass" has too often been seen as an act of individual discipline or devotion that would save one's soul. But more attention needs to be paid to every celebration of the Eucharist's social mission for believers to replicate the love of God, "which has been poured into our hearts through the Holy Spirit that has been given to us." This is the love that responds to transgression, not with wrath, but with forgiveness and strategies for reconciliation (Rom 5:6–11).

Belief in the forgiveness of sins, as affirmed in the Creed, expands our circle of concern to include even those guilty of crimes. Such an extension "can be jump started by a vivid narrative," writes political philosopher Martha Nussbaum.[68] And what more vivid a narrative can we find than Jesus' dialogue and parable responding to Peter's mathematical formula for forgiveness, "As many as seven times? Jesus said to him, Not seven times. But, I tell you, seventy-seven times."[69] What follows next in the Creed fleshes out how faith ultimately responds to the wound of mortality itself and looks to a "rebirth/new age" (Matt 19:28).

I look for the resurrection of the dead, and the life of the world-to-come. Amen.

Unlike the notion of the soul's natural immortality, resurrection of the body is understood as only the prelude to the "world-to-come," a reordered cosmos where injustice no longer prevails. In essence, both expectations summon the faithful to hope a society into existence where life always comes from dying, where love wins out over hate, where justice and peace weave the fabric of life for all the living.

---

68. Nussbaum, *Political Emotions*, 265.

69. The NRSV offers the alternative translation of the phrase in Matthew 18:22 as "seventy times seven times," which is adopted in other translations. Merton links Jesus' response to unlimited forgiveness with his teaching on nonviolence, which "takes into account . . . the non-final state of all relationships among men, for non-violence seeks to change relationships that are evil into others that are good, or at least less bad" (*Gandhi*, 13).

Extending the Narrative

When parsing the "resurrection of the dead," I face the greatest challenge to opening a contemporary perspective on the Creed's overall narrative. Both this belief and the following expectation of "the life of the world-to-come" look to an amorphous future, an unrealized hope unanchored in any past event. But without this companion affirmation, this "resurrection" falls into literalism's maw, which swallows hope rather than enlivens it today. The one cannot be understood apart from the other.

With this in view, I will discuss them sequentially, insisting all the while that we cannot take refuge in any simple, literal meanings attaching to them. Yet, since we have already professed Christ's resurrection, our looked-for resurrection must comport with that belief as well. And, as in the case of Christ, this idea of living again on the other side of death must be distinguished from Plato's teaching on the immortality of the soul. Last century, the New Testament scholar Oscar Cullmann wrote an essay, *Immortality of the Soul*,[70] that contrasted the accounts of Socrates's trial and death with Jesus' passion and death on the cross. Controversial at the time, its contrast of these opposing scenes might help move our inquiry forward.

Ever the philosopher, as related in Plato's *Apology*, Socrates surmised either that death was a final end of life or that his soul would survive and live in another form. This allowed him to drink the prescribed hemlock with equanimity. Plato does not seem to have imposed his own, more cosmic vision of judgment on his mentor. But Jesus, both in his garden agony and on the cross, faced death with *both* terror and willing acceptance. Though he trusted himself to the Father, the accounts of his passion and death do not shrink from (or negate) his sharing human mortality in its feared outcome, being cut off finally from the land of the living. As we saw earlier, his death was not faked. It was real, as all of ours will someday be.

But beyond the terror, Jesus brought to his encounter with dying a belief that had been growing in the Pharisaic or early rabbinic strain of Judaism: God's faithfulness guaranteed just persons

---

70. Cullman, *Immortality of the Soul*.

a genuine second act. Like the law-keeping Jews in the centuries before him, Jesus looked forward to God's restoration of the people Israel in all their fullness via "resurrection." As we saw earlier, 2 Maccabees made explicit a belief that God would restore martyrs to life in the age-to-come (7:1-29).

In the same way that it functioned for Jesus, resurrection became the moral and imaginative framework into which early believers fit their experience of Jesus beyond his death on the cross. I argued earlier that resurrection from the dead does not mean that Jesus' cadaver was resuscitated. Equivalently, Christian belief that Jesus was but "the firstborn within a large family" (Rom 8:29) has nothing to do with popular entertainment's fascination with the undead. Nor does it mean that Plato's other, idealized, nonmaterial world exists to welcome the souls of the dead to a heavenly bliss unburdened by suffering for all eternity. Despite the suggestive power of the art of souls ascending—I'm thinking of all the baroque paintings in church domes—this creedal affirmation does not literally call on believers to look forward to a non-terrestrial sphere of existence populated by bodyless souls. Resurrection, either of the firstborn Christ or his many brothers and sisters, remains a metaphor steeped in history but inexact in its meaning.[71]

Even in Paul's explicit teaching about the world-to-come (in Hebrew, the *'ōlam haba*, also spoken of as "the age-to-come"), there remains an unresolved tension. He firmly believed that salvation was dawning now in this age. But the process begun with Christ's new life would not be complete until a further consummation (what Matthew, as mentioned earlier, termed the "rebirth"). The apostle used explicit pictures of the archangel's trumpet that would announce the risen Jesus' return when both the living and the dead would join in communion with him. When he relied on this common apocalyptic imagery, he was emphasizing to skeptical Greek believers in Corinth that salvation involved the "body,"

---

71. When exactly the phrase, as found in the text of the Apostles' Creed (in Latin), *vitam aeternam* (everlasting life) came to be used as opposed to the Nicene Greek *zōēn tou mellontos aiōnos* (the life of the world-/age-to-come) is unknown. But, as I argued earlier, the latter corresponds much more closely to the expectation of Jesus, Paul, and the early church.

not just the soul. Like a seed sown in the ground that blooms wholly differently, so life in a "heavenly body" would have only a bare resemblance to what went before. To imagine the end of one age, and the arrival of another (1 Cor 10:11) that he saw coming, he engaged in a paradox. "Spiritual bodies" would populate the "new creation" or the reign of God (1 Cor 15:36–41). Nowhere does he countenance any *naturally* immortal souls dwelling in an ethereal heaven.

As hard as this viewpoint might be for churchgoers to grasp, the immortality of the soul has little support in the writings of the New Testament. Earlier I noted that the apocryphal Wisdom of Solomon, which emerged from Greek-speaking Jews in Hellenistic Egypt, took refuge in God's present vindication of the souls of the just. It is a favorite text in funeral liturgies: "The souls of the just are in the hands of God, and no torment shall touch them. They seemed in the eyes of the foolish to be dead . . . but they are at peace" (3:1–3). But even here, the full vindication of the persecuted just lies *in the future reversal of fate* when "they will govern nations and rule over peoples and the LORD shall reign over them forever" (v. 8). This triumph lies ahead, as Jesus also affirmed. So collapsing a dynamic, temporal notion of the coming kingdom into an ever-present, otherworldly realm does not do justice to the Christian story.

So the Creed's looking forward to "the resurrection of the dead" corresponds to a future event when the reign of God that Jesus announced will be revealed to "all flesh." The promise remind us of Isaiah's vision where "all the nations shall stream" to the mountain of the Lord's house (Isa 2:2) The scenario of the parousia or reappearance of the Messiah remains a gripping one. Again, it has fueled the imaginations of artists, musicians, and writers for millennia. But, in truth, it corresponds to no possible, or actual, geographical, astral, or geophysical reality in the fabric of the cosmos as we now know it to have existed for multiple billions of years. This picture arose from a visionary, but physically naïve, view of the entire universe common for several millennia. But, after Galileo, Newton, Einstein, and others began unraveling the actual shape of the cosmos and its physical principles, we cannot interpret this hoped-for "event" to occur as it was once imagined. It speaks to us still, but how can we appropriate it in its prophetic, yet nonliteral, sense?

Certainly, not by dismissing either resurrection or the world-to-come as mere fantasy. They remain part of our profession of faith, but faith requires us to engage them via a dynamic analogy, not in a static restatement of an untranslatable, mythic event. Let me explain what I mean by "dynamic analogy."[72] The story of Moses's salvation from death dynamically reimagined Noah's rescue of all living things in the "ark." His mother used a vessel of the same name, "plastered with bitumen and pitch" setting him adrift in the Nile (Exod 2:3).

So too, the events of the exodus or flight from Egypt, whether they occurred historically or not, became the template against which Jewish refugees, freed from Babylon centuries later, understood their journey through the wilderness and return to Jerusalem. The former story birthed the latter and gave substance to an unlikely political outcome. It remains, to this day, a powerfully dynamic analogy for a plethora of liberation movements, instilling hope and engendering strategies for oppressed people to move toward greater freedom.

So too, Exodus's manna in the desert spawned the image, in Deuteronomy, of "every word that comes forth from the mouth of God." Still later, in the Wisdom of Solomon, manna became heavenly bread that possessed everyone's favorite tastes, not the bitter hoarfrost the Hebrews in the desert consumed. Yet again, the Fourth Gospel reimagines Jesus as the Word come into the world as heavenly manna, the bread of life. In other words, pregnant events, persons, and acts of faith never confine themselves to

---

72. Sanders explains, "By *dynamic analogy* we mean re-presenting the tradition, consciously identifying with the character or characters in the tradition most *representative* of the new hearers or readers. [It] presupposes the view that believing communities are essentially pilgrim folk needing the canonical challenge to move on and take another step on the pilgrimage toward the goal God's story or history envisages" (*Canon and Community*, 70–71).

a single meaning. They become templates for recasting and finding new promises and possibilities in later events.

As I argued just above, the "resurrection of the dead" cannot be grasped by faith without pairing it with "the life of the world-to-come." The twinned phrases reflected early Judaism's belief that "this world" had become corrupt. Under the thrall of evil forces, "the powers and principalities" that Paul spoke of, these "mighty ones" would be toppled from their thrones in the age of the Messiah. In the visions of the book of Revelation, "Babylon" (i.e., Rome's imperial domination) would soon collapse and be replaced by a kingdom, the Holy City, where God would dwell in perfect communion with humanity.

The parties behind the Dead Sea Scrolls also looked forward to such a restored world. It would come about after a final battle when Michael the Archangel—or perhaps Melchizedek and a host of angels—would destroy the *Kittim*—their designation for the occupying Gentiles. All of these beliefs foresaw and looked forward to the reordering of the political and social order. God's reign would replace the injustice and oppression that burdened the poor, the lowly in society, the starving masses, the victims of war, all those crying out for justice.

This sense of impending crisis undergirded Jesus' teaching that "the time is at hand," (Mark 1:15) and Paul's refashioned belief that "the time is short" (1 Cor 7:29). The old order, also represented by Herod's Temple, would soon be rebuilt or replaced by God. Both Jesus' prophecy of Jerusalem's destruction, and the warning to his accusers that they would soon see "the Son of Man coming on the clouds of heaven" (Mark 14:62), signaled that the old world was nearing its end. Well into the next century, Christians continued to defend the truth of the prophecy that the coming day of the Lord would bring about "the new heavens and the new earth" where God's justice would reside (2 Pet 3:13). Again, these apocalyptic beliefs did not countenance God's provoking a violent conflict to achieve this. The kingdom would come, not as the result of "kingdom rising against kingdom," but as "a thief in the night," a revelation of the cosmic Christ that spelled the end of politics as a perpetually violent struggle for power and dominion.

But this belief in the "world-to-come" nowhere refers to a heavenly realm populated by souls who had once lived in this world but who now enjoyed disembodied life in another, nonphysical and eternal one. At most, there is a sense that, in this in-between time, those who have died "in the Lord" would not miss out on the final redemption. Thus the "paradise" promised to the "good thief" (Luke 23:43) is a place of waiting populated by the souls of those "under the altar" who had been slain for their testimony (Rev 6:9). As "martyrs," they give witness and cry out for the final redemption. They do not enjoy heavenly bliss as souls in an eternal afterlife. This could not be clearer than in the concluding vision of Revelation—surely the most thoroughly apocalyptic book in the New Testament. As above, the world-to-come occurs when God brings about the "new heaven and new earth" of believers' hope (21:1). The new temple and Jerusalem from above symbolize the divine and human communion revealed to John the Seer of Revelation as the final outcome of Jesus' death, resurrection, and enthronement.

Elaborated by this early precursor of Hollywood's sci-fi blockbusters, all Revelation's visions fill out the simple prayer in the mouth of Jesus: "thy kingdom come, thy will be done on earth." Transposed, then, by Jesus' own Passover from death to life, this last book of the New Testament's final prayer begs "*Maranatha*," "Come, Lord Jesus"—just as Paul himself and the Aramaic Didache's early liturgical text also prayed. These visions and prayers all express the early communities' pleas for the full redemption of the creation that was originally labeled "good" by the world's Creator (Gen 1:31).

But how can any of these scenarios relate to believers' lives and deaths in the twenty-first century? The whole "biblical worldview" with its one-sun cosmos, for all its poetic power, can no longer be an adequate frame, by itself, for Christian faith or hope. Sentimental affirmations of an "afterlife" that tell us that those who have died "are in a better place" really do not measure up to the promise. They neither translate the canonical vision of the New Testament nor can they adequately represent the unfolding mystery of our edgeless universe. Translating "the world-to-come" as "eternal life" foreshortens the Creed's vibrant echo of the biblical hope and promise of a wholly renewed *'ōlam* [Hebrew], *aiōn* [Greek], or *saeculum* [Latin]—a new age/world-to-come.

The story of how this happened can't be easily told, but suffice it to say that this world's history marched on. In the face of what Christians experienced and what scholars term the "delay of the parousia," or Jesus' triumphant return, they increasingly took refuge in Neoplatonism's scheme that a spiritual realm, higher and better, exists above this earthly, material one. Having quit this mortal coil, the souls of those judged to be just following their death migrate to a different plane of existence apart from the created but not-yet-redeemed world "here below." To accord with a literal reading of the parable of the sheep and the goats (Matt 25:31–46), some scenarios forecast a final redo of the individual judgment that each soul received at death. But, again, collapsing "the life of the world-to-come" into an atemporal "everlasting life" hollows out the challenge it issues collectively to all believers across the ages.

A twentieth-century Christian Platonist, C. S. Lewis, in his gripping tale *The Great Divorce*, virtually recaps this mythic picture of a heavenly afterlife from Plato's *Phaedo* (his dialogue *On the Soul*). As a parable of final judgment, it has enormous and lasting attraction, but there is nothing specifically Christian about it. A hybrid doctrine, the natural immortality of the soul, captured there steps back from the hope of a reborn world by making the end point of salvation unworldly, ethereal, and individual.

It absolutizes Matthew 25's parable of judgment where "eternal punishment" and "eternal life" seem to describe hell and heaven as alien to the created world. Yet, as I argued previously, this parable, so different from others featuring a king or master, reveals a radical, and unexpected, solidarity between a royal judge and the lowliest of his subjects. Its power comes from the surprise or shock that both the virtuous and the wicked experience when they grasp what life in the world-to-come will be like. Not unlike Luke's version of the Beatitudes, one's future fate in the kingdom depends on how one treats the poor and the hungry in the here and now. Still, it remains a *parable* seeking to move listeners to moral action in their individual, social, and political lives. Considering it a literal, cosmic doctrine about a hellish or heavenly afterlife, and building an entire moral superstructure upon it, twists the message out of its actual context.

The same needs to be said about Luke's parable known as Lazarus and Dives (the rich man) in 16:19–31. Using a mythic great "chasm" between the bosom of Abraham and a place of torment for the uncaring rich, the parable issues a this-worldly challenge about riches. Jesus had already counseled risking the moral hazard of using "dishonest wealth" to assure a place in what is often translated "eternal homes" (16:9) to sound like a traditional view of heaven. But an alternate sense of the phrase *aiōnios skēnas* suggests "dwellings in the new age," i.e., where wealth no longer measures a person's worth.

The common view of heaven and hell, as alternate spiritual spheres of existence, arose from combining two very different worldviews: a Greek notion of the soul's spiritual existence grafted onto an earthly place for refuse, Gehenna, the fiery garbage dump outside the gates of Jerusalem: "where their worm never dies, and the fire is never quenched" (Mark 9:48). This was then spiritualized via early Judaism's expectation of judgment as catalyst for the redemption and re-creation of the cosmos. In fact, it is certain that neither Jesus, Paul, nor the Creed had this later, spiritualized scenario of heaven or hell (as later pictured) in mind when they envisioned the dawning of the world-to-come. By contrast, the mythic wording of the Creed promotes a lively expectation that contains truth value beyond any literal notion that "salvation" consists of the soul's persistence after death in a state of reward or punishment.

To recap, the Creed's full narrative of salvation asserts that the Christ story, in its fullness, reveals a cosmic process by which "in the fullness of time" the Son of Man will return, sort out good from evil, and establish God's justice as the basis of a renewed creation. In this mythic scenario, those faithful alive at this second coming would be joined with all those who had come before them who would then rise to enjoy communion with all the saints and "be with the Lord forever" (1 Thess 4:17). But if we are honest, these visions of salvation, as powerfully poetic as they are, pose a real challenge for contemporary belief. But they also express a promise that surpasses any literal description of the future fate of the soul. Their mythic shape comes from the same imaginative stock as the Genesis creation narratives and the visions of the prophet Isaiah. As creation myths and re-creation hopes, they resonate with the rhythms of death and of life for the entire cosmos. As myths, they do not conform to any past or present configuration of the physical world as we know it or of an imagined completely nonmaterial, heavenly one.

Instead, they summon the faithful to hope a society into existence where life always comes from dying, where love wins out over hate, where justice and peace weave the fabric of life for all the living. Everything that believers do, respond to, or create is meant to mirror the goodness, peace, and justice of the reign or the kingdom of God that Jesus himself prayed would "come to earth." These articles of the Creed summon believers to active communion with the whole of creation, with those who have lived before us, with those who share life with us today, and with the billions who will take our place in the river of time. Their cosmic shape dwarfs and renders secondary any one individual's expectation of his or her soul's continuing a non-bodily existence at the end of this life.

What then of heaven and the afterlife? Have we outgrown belief in an immediate post-death, soul-only communion with God, the saints, and our ancestors in a heavenly realm? Certainly, the most common form of Christian belief tends to assert such an image. But I would have to answer "Yes," if faith is taken to posit a bodyless family reunion for all eternity. Or if this belief sees heaven as a blissful way station for souls awaiting a reunion with a "spiritual" body as St. Paul mythologized it. But also "No" if we can enlarge our vision to encompass the entire sweep of the biblical revelation. For the Bible's story (which encapsulates Christianity's "good news") reveals that our personal and social narratives are entwined within a cosmic story, one that complicates our notions of the past, present, and future.

We have seen that the Creed uses a past/present/future framework to tell its story. But the mystery behind its story structure defies Aristotle's "arrow of time," where the past has disappeared, the present is fleeting, and the future has as yet no existence. In the early twentieth century, Einstein's space-time continuum messed with our everyday notions of time and space. But long before, "God's time" was known to lie outside our normal categories of what we experience.

For evidence, look no further than the Fourth Gospel and its take on rebirth and life. Though sharing much of the narrative structure of the other Gospels, this document repositions resurrection and the life of the world-to-come from a vague future into the ongoing, ever-present now. "Rebirth" is not just something that is awaited; it happens in the now of the believer's present. "Life" is not bifurcated by our biological living and dying. Present from the beginning, it shines its light on humanity, even upon our manifold failures to grasp that luminous gift. Life happens when love and forgiveness animate the church and its members. Life, like love, names God's presence to and within creation, simultaneously manifest in the past-present-future of all that exists. In this Gospel's atemporal perspective, even "resurrection" happens at the moment of the Messiah's being "lifted up" in death on the cross. "Salvation" occurs when those "born again of water and the spirit" share the bread of life, when believers abide in the kind of love by which Jesus laid down his life for his friends.

In other words, this Gospel's take on life and death shares significant similarities with experiences of the apostle Paul, and many mystics since, whose union with Christ in the now of his suffering also shared in his being raised up in glory. Although Paul's temporal framework remained anchored in a vibrant expectation of world-change, he also had supratemporal experiences of Christ's life in his very person. Along with other New Testament writers, he understood his work, the founding of communities of believers, as divinely present beforehand—even from the foundation of the world (Eph 1:4). In other words, our notions about past, present, and future pale when measured against the limitless scope of God's creative presence, in Word and in Spirit, to all of creation.

The notion of heaven as an eternal afterlife only developed when the prophets' call for justice, Jesus' own expectation of a temple "not made by hands," and even the early church's yearning for the return of Jesus, waned over time. Yet all of these ancient mythic expectations arose because people experienced a limited three-tiered cosmos of heaven-earth-hell. We cannot gainsay them as if they were not appropriate to their time and culture. But they cannot be taken as prescriptive or descriptive of a shadow universe of immaterial beings gathered around God's throne singing "Hallelujah." As majestic, poetic, artistic, and musical scenarios (think Handel's "Blessing and honor, power and glory . . ." at the end of *Messiah*), they move us aesthetically and spiritually. But they must be transcended to grasp what they are about.

The human imagination, itself a gift of our evolved consciousness, translated experiences of the Transcendent into Abraham's sacrifice, Moses on the mountain, Isaiah's vision, and countless others. Jesus' transfiguration, Lazarus' revival, Peter's vision in Acts 10, Paul's ascent to the third heaven, the Beloved Disciple's testimony, and John the Seer's vision of the Alpha and Omega in Revelation—these all tell us that the "world-to-come" is always already present as well as not fully realized.

Praying for the coming of the kingdom of God "on earth as in heaven" challenges us to anchor our faith lives and hopes in enacting God's justice in the here and now. Sharing now in the communion of the Holy Spirit, as a "pledge/guarantee" of a new creation, requires that we *do justice* in every society where the dignity of all creation is denied or taken for granted. Jesus' blessing promised to the poor, the meek, the lowly, and those who hunger for justice cannot be postponed to a "by-and-by" afterlife. God's presence in blessing happens whenever the mighty are cast down from their thrones, the lowly are lifted up, the hungry are filled with good things, and the self-satisfied rich are sent away empty.

CHAPTER 4

Faith as Doing Justice

Reciting the Creed at this stage of my life continues my personal quest to understand and share in a communion that calls me outside of myself. It commits me to care for creation, to act for generations to come and to promote an expanded view of justice as the surest way to affirm the gift that my life and my faith have been.

BY WAY OF CONCLUDING my inquiry, my faith affirms that "heaven" (originally another Divine Name) is already present in our communion with all those living and dead and in our discovering God's indwelling among all created things. But because our natural, biological lives share in this indwelling, we believe our graced relationship with the divine extends beyond our limited, individual life spans. As St. Paul says: "Both in life and in death we are the [risen] Lord's" (Rom 14:8). Today, we know that we "human" beings (literally, beings of the earth) were created from the molecular matter of the cosmos and will forever remain part of it. In the biome that we share, the very dust of the stars has become self-conscious and aware of its responsibility for the gift of the created world we have inherited. As part of this awareness, we recognize that the entire cosmos is an ever-unfolding mystery that has tended, from its earliest beginning, toward a yet unrealized future. While we are among the living, we have the awesome and awe-filled opportunity to practice thanksgiving and blessing ("Eucharist") in the way we worship and to be strengthened by it to seek the kingdom of God and its justice. When we die, we do not face extinction as modern secular thinkers confidently proclaim. We remain bonded with the matter from which we came. But we also continue to hold an unrepeatable place in the great chain of being. As persons who have enjoyed (and been burdened by) the gift of conscious selfhood, we shall not have lived for ourselves alone. And as a person who lived in union with Christ, we do not die alone. Rather, we fall asleep in the Lord and enter that "great cloud of witnesses" to the power of faith that calls believers to join in the common human vocation to live justly. When the liturgy prays, "Eternal rest grant unto them, O Lord, and let perpetual light shine upon them," we affirm that our labors have ceased. Yet, when the memory or record of our lives fade into dust, we still remain sharers in an evolutionary drama whose end only arrives "when God will be all in all" (1 Cor 15:28).

But we can ask whether, in this chastened scenario of redemption, Christians enjoy any special privilege or reward for their faithful lives. What about all those familiar tropes about distinguishing between good and evil, of separating good people from bad in some future final judgment? I have argued that these ancient parables follow a pattern developed by the writing prophets of Israel. In them, courtroom scenes abound. The people are sued for violating their covenant with God. Warning them of the consequences of their perfidy, selfishness, injustice, and self-serving religious practices, the prophets pleaded for a moral and political revolution. But their promises of reward and threats of punishment always remained rooted in earth. They pressed for a just society, hoped for a just king, raged at arrogant leaders, and promised the community's reestablishment after exile.

Only afterward were these warnings and hopes inflated into a more universal, yet individualized, schema of reward or punishment that followed one's death here below. We should credit these cries for justice and threats of punishment as heuristic fictions and, as such, they will always function as motivations for individual, social, and political reform. They call out to conscience, that inner awareness that "good is to be pursued and evil avoided," which some will seek to silence but never be able to extinguish.

At base, a life of prayer and living for the kingdom of heaven to come to earth and for God's will to be done commits believers to struggle toward a future human community where the justice of God will reside more fully. Today our institutions of science, government, and religion are all emerging from self-serving ignorance about technologies and their Faustian shadow side. We, the living, have no right to squander the goods of the earth and use them for our own thriving or enjoyment alone. Today, our moral compass can be said to have evolved to include more of humanity, and nature itself, in our circle of concern.

So if I look forward to any reward for my faith and work for justice, it will be found in a world-to-come for my grandchildren, and their grandchildren, for as long as humanity manages to hang on to the awesome gifts that both "Nature and Nature's God" have bestowed. So-called "transhumanists" strive to invent new medical and other technologies for prolonging their own lives indefinitely, locking in a vast inequality that deprives the world's people hungering for some present share in happiness, dignity, and freedom. Others believe in the inevitability of "the Singularity," a point at which an evolved superintelligence will end the human era.[1] Science fiction or not, we today can *do justice* humbly, working to raise up marginalized people to the full stature of humanity in which we believe divinity also resides. In a stranger-than-strange universe we live not for ourselves alone but partners in the Mystery of gratuitous love and reconciling justice.

For, beneath all our pretenses, we know that our very lives come to us as unmerited gifts, even when we suffer evil or we commit it, when we experience disaster or death. For its part, moral evil, which only humans are capable of committing, actually mirrors the freedom of the physical world in all its randomness and

---

1. An exhaustive description of the concept(s), proponents, and opponents appears in https://en.wikipedia.org/wiki/Technological_singularity.

contingency. The COVID pandemic resulted, ironically, from lifeless viruses that have struggled for dominance over living organisms for uncountable eons. They have always needed living creatures to replicate and survive. In the past, tragedies and plagues multiplied for millennia because neither science nor religion had any knowledge of bacteria or viruses and people suffered defenselessly. Even today, what scientists have sussed out about them has failed to protect millions because of malevolent ignorance and ingrained poverty. And for all this time, an all-suffering divinity has accompanied the pregnant matter of the universe in its coming to birth and in its evolving struggles. As I have argued, if nature were not itself in all its orderly chaos, we would only be playacting in a predetermined dance of life versus death, unfree and ultimately unloved. Accepting the world as it is only ups the ante for us as human beings, individually and collectively, to negotiate random contingencies from earthquakes, storms, and the like, all the while understanding our own complicity in making this world less habitable.

Only caricatures of the biblical revelation portray our lives as characters in God's puppet show. Sadly, bad theology then compounds these caricatures with its own schemes of how God plays tit for tat with rebellious humans, dangling the ultimate reward but weighing any slip-ups as meriting eternal exile. Today, any portrayal of religion that promotes this portrait severs the Creator from the myriad human beings who have barely gotten to share the gift of life. Children in the millions have died, victims of disease, neglect, and ignorance. Untold masses have fallen in senseless warfare, suffered ancient as well as newer forms of terrorism. We dare not embrace any system of cosmology or morality that assigns so many victims of nature's own random injustice or humanity's selfish violence to the cause of divine retribution or indifference. For Christians, the cross and the crucifix remain vibrant symbols of God's sharing with humanity the cost of an imperfect creation.

The narrative embedded in the Creed captures a much larger, more cosmic tale of Love as the beginning and end of all things beyond suffering and death. But the ultimate and ever-present correlate of that Love resides in God's justice. Enacted by repentance, and carried out via mercy, forgiveness, and reconciliation, this justice is the highest calling of all who make the Creed their own. Without twinning Love and justice, religious faith only disguises humanity's narcissistic self-involvement. Its version of hope means little to nothing that benefits any persons except the winners of life's economic lottery

So reciting the Creed as part of a celebration of the sacraments of baptism and the Eucharist at this stage of my life continues my personal quest to understand and share in a communion that calls me outside of myself. It commits me to care for creation, to act for generations to come, and to promote this expanded view of justice as the surest way to affirm the gift that my life has been. If my engagement with the story embedded in the Creed, and its deeper meaning, may help to disengage Christianity from a too-narrow and uncatholic self-awareness, then I shall not have toiled in vain. I can only hope to suffer the loss of my individual life as I have lived it: redeemed and forgiven for my pettiness and selfishness, yet loved despite them. I strive, despite my own final ignorance of the great unknown, in faith to accept that love, to let go of my grip and make room for other members of Christ's body to take up the continuing struggle for a more just creation.

Appendix A

BEHIND SEVERAL OF THE images of sacrifice in the New Testament lies the feast of the Passover, the very backdrop to the trials and execution of Jesus. But each of the writers uses the poetic force of the images in distinct ways, undermining any sense that they denote Jesus as a sacrificial victim. For his part, Paul exhorts his Corinthian congregation to shed sexual immorality—a lifestyle for which Corinth was infamous—by rhetorically employing two images: matzah and the sacrifice of a lamb. Linked together loosely in Exodus 12, the apostle poetically transforms the day observed as a "perpetual ordinance" (v. 14) into a new/moral way of life that he has championed. For, now that "Christ, our paschal lamb, has been sacrificed," a new feast can be celebrated, not with old matzah, but with "the unleavened bread of sincerity and truth" (1 Cor 5:7-8). Here, Paul uses "sacrifice" and "feast" as metaphors for Christ's death and its unlikely outcome to convince his congregation to outgrow their libertinism. He makes no claim that anyone put Christ to death as a literal sacrificial victim. Instead, his death on the cross, pictured in the same letter as a ruse to fool the ruling powers (2:8; see Eph 6:12), become a goad for moral transformation. His congregants "feast" when they themselves pass-over from immorality to truth. As he would also assure them, this age of the world, in which they have lived, is already ceding to a new one (10:11). Wrenching the image from the context of persuading his followers how to act in a time of "impending crisis" (7:26) makes the text slip its metaphorical mooring.

Appendix A

As we will see, metaphors of sacrifice were employed to emphasize a startling and stark paradox: divine goodness has emerged from the malicious actions of humans. At the same time, none of the authors had to weave their tale afresh. They possessed threads taken from old, familiar textual cloth that lay at hand and could be made new. Employing several familiar narrative patterns, they rewove them in a new revelation of God's love. Paul uses one of these when he riffs upon Abraham's faith in Genesis 22, making it say something quite different from the original. In Romans, God follows Abraham's example rather than Abraham obeying God's command. Here God does not withhold "his own Son but gave him up for all of us" (Rom 8:32). This strange reversal stems from the apostle's linking the tales of two "only sons." The likely source came from an early postbiblical rereading of Genesis, particularly the story known as "The Binding/Sacrifice of Isaac." In it, Abraham's son does not just follow along together with his father, but willingly offers himself to be a lamb for the sacrifice. In doing this, the son earned a share in the promise to Abraham of offspring "as numerous as the stars of heaven" (Gen 22:17).

Like Isaac, then, Jesus had joined in his father's act of offering.[1] In his death, Jesus becomes the assurance that "neither death, nor life, nor angels, nor rulers, nor things present, nor things to come, nor powers, nor height, nor depth, nor anything else in all creation, will be able to separate us from the love of God (Rom 8:38–39). As we saw in 1 Corinthians, Jesus as Passover sacrifice is not about death, but about love. It derives from the same stock of metaphorical images that reconfigure death into a promise of life.

Earlier in Romans "blood" functions as a powerful metaphor of God's grace through Jesus when Paul speaks of God's peculiar form of justice. In the face of the universal sin of both Jews and Gentiles, Paul's gospel proposed an anomaly. Faith alone grasps that God's grace "put forward" Jesus' death as a '*ilastērion* (a means or place of atonement). The result: forgiveness with no distinction

---

1. Vermes surmises, "The image of the self-immolation of Isaac, dated in early post-biblical Jewish tradition to Passover day on 15 Nisan, must have been lurking in Paul's subconscious" (*Christian Beginnings*, 103).

Appendix A

between Jew and Gentile (3:21–26). This play upon the once yearly pouring of the blood of a lamb on the altar in the holy of holies will figure more prominently in Hebrews. It represents a metaphorical valuation of the death of Jesus within the traditional understanding of the sprinkling or pouring of blood for purification (cf. the rabbinical bYoma 5a, Heb 9:22). But literalizing Jesus' blood as possessing totemic power to wipe sin away borders on magic. His death, symbolized via an ancient belief that "life is in the blood" (Lev 17:11), becomes, in faith, not a sacrificial loss, but a gift of life.

The same analogy is further threaded through the lens of the Passover in the Fourth Gospel. There, Jesus lays down his life for his friends—but takes it up again (John 10:17), just as Isaac's life is "restored" by God. In affirming this reversal from death to life, the evangelist portrays Christ's death as *equivalent* in its impact to two wonders of old: Abraham's "sacrifice" (cf. Heb 11:19)[2] and the sacrificial gift of the Pasch that freed Israel of old.[3] Then, on the strength of this second analogy, this gospel actually restructures the timetable of events surrounding Jesus' death in a way that contradicts the other three gospel accounts. In John 13–17, the "Last Supper" is not a Passover meal as in Matthew, Mark, and Luke. It takes place on the eve of the feast so that Jesus dies on the cross at the same time that the Passover lambs are being sacrificed in the temple.[4] "None of his bones shall be broken," from the original Passover ritual (Exod 12:46), had foreshadowed how the soldiers would treat Jesus' body. Uniquely in this Gospel Jesus dies, in no way either "abandoned" nor a sacrificial victim, but as victor on the cross (19:30). Neither the apostle, nor the evangelist, allows us to claim that either Isaac or Jesus suffered death as a ritual "offering" to any deity.

---

2. The same tradition likely lies behind this verse in Hebrews that says of Abraham's faith: "He considered the fact that God is able even to raise someone from the dead—and figuratively speaking, he did receive him back."

3. Vermes writes, "According to the oldest Jewish tradition on the subject (Jub. 17:15), the quasi-immolation of Isaac took place on 15 Nisan, the date of the future feast of Passover" (*Christian Beginnings*, 125).

4. Vermes, *Christian Beginnings*, 124.

Appendix A

In another feasting context, where eating and new life occur in John 6, the true bread from heaven is given by God as Jesus' body to be eaten and his blood to be drunk. But no association is made of this "sign" of heavenly bread (John 6:32) with Passover or any sacrificial death. Rather his life is heavenly nourishment, God's gift for "life to the world" (v. 33). The living water that Jesus gives in 4:14 and the bread that came down from heaven both signify a new access to life in the resurrected age (*aiōn* ushered in "on the last day" of this age, 6:54). Especially with this Gospel, literalism diminishes, rather than enhances, the poetic truth value in its many expressive signs.

Several other uses of sacrificial images and terms have also been misperceived in two-dimensional, literal terms. A number of them occur in the Letter to the Hebrews. But, in that letter, the only reference to Passover concerns Moses' faith in observing it (11:28). Instead, Hebrews styles a complex, even midrashic, homily on analogy with the Day of Atonement. This provides a different palette upon which to paint vibrant images of Christ's death and transformation. I believe that giving it some special attention will help us understand how thoroughly metaphorical—and not literal—the notion of sacrifice registers in the New Testament.

Hebrews alone imaginatively recasts Jesus' historically prophetic life and mission not only as a royal, but also as a priestly ministry. Capturing Jesus of Nazareth's own prophesy that Herod's temple would soon be replaced by one "not made by hands" (cf. Mark 14:58[5]/Heb 9:11), the author thoroughly reworked this historical hope into a supra-historical scenario. In the fashion of a midrash, the letter stitched together two previously unrelated divine addresses: Psalm 2's "You are my son" with Psalm 110's "You are a

---

5. Though this is "false testimony" given against Jesus in his trial (v. 47), there is good reason to believe Jesus did make such a threat. This is echoed in the testimony given against Stephen in Acts 6:14: "we have heard him say that this Jesus of Nazareth will destroy this place" (in Greek *topon* is code language for the temple). John 2:19 christologizes the threat: "Destroy this temple, and in three days I will raise it up." E. P. Sanders (*Jesus and Judaism*, 75) gives this careful hypothesis: "Jesus predicted (or threatened) the destruction of the Temple and carried out an action symbolic of its destruction . . ."

Appendix A

priest forever in the line of Melchizedek" (Heb 5:5–6).[6] By doing this, the author proclaims Jesus, said to be of David's royal lineage, to have become exalted as a "new and eternal High Priest," whose passage into the divine presence pioneered the covenant that Jeremiah prophesied (8:8–12). Jesus is portrayed as "resembling" Melchizedek (7:15), but his ancient precursor never entered the holy of holies. Rather, the rhetorical move in Hebrews dissociates Jesus' "priestly" role from his literally offering a literal sacrifice. The priest-king himself in Genesis 14:8 only "brought out bread and wine" to Abraham as a hospitality gift; he does not offer sacrifice as was later asserted by anti-Jewish apologetics.

Hebrews' very distinct picture-world even avoids declaring Christ "risen from the dead." Rather, Jesus' life, death, and exaltation is portrayed *as a cosmic hero's journey: from life as "a son" among the angels, to life in solidarity with his brothers and sisters of flesh, through the "loud cries and tears" of his suffering and obedient death, to his passage through the "veil" (of his flesh, a metaphor of his death, Heb 10:20), into the inner shrine or Holy Place where God dwells (compare Phil 2:6–11)*. In this highly mythological scenario, actual sacrificial worship through the outpouring of blood on the Day of Atonement is rendered obsolete. Christ's passage "once and for all" into God's glory accomplished what had only been an earthly premonition—worship in the pre-temple imitation of God's sanctuary (8:5). In "these last days," those now called "holy partners in a heavenly calling" (3:1) worship, not via sacrifice, but via the *network of spiritual relationships* that constitutes a "sacrifice of praise" (13:1–16). Worshippers now can "approach the throne of grace" (a vibrant metaphor originally describing the altar in the temple's holy of holies, 4:16) in a relationship with God that transforms both the content and mode of worship.[7] In sum,

---

6. Boyarin generalizes that "the fundamental moment of all these midrashic forms is precisely the very cocitation of several verses." In addition, "those midrashic texts which are *only* quotations strung together . . . would be, on my theory, the very ideal type of midrash" (*Intertextuality*, 29; 137n24).

7. The inference here is that believers can do what, once, only the high priest could do, i.e., enter the holy of holies where Christ has gone before them. In Hebrews 9:5, the throne of grace appears as the "mercy seat" (*'ilastērion*).

Appendix A

Christ's "priesthood" is a metaphor for his unending mediatory life in communion with God, something only achieved by his sharing the universal fate of humanity: suffering and death. But victimhood of any stripe is ruled out. The blood that he carries into God's very presence stands for his mortality, not his being slain as a victim. Turning this mythic scenario of world-change into a promise of individual reward in a heavenly afterlife misreads the letter.

Lastly, just as Hebrews sought to comfort and encourage those who "have not yet resisted to the point of shedding blood (12:4), other persecuted victims looked to the visionary image of the Lamb in the book of Revelation. The work's exceptionally graphic use of metaphors, on first reading, might lend themselves to identifying Jesus as an explicitly sacrificial victim. But examining two prominent instances will disabuse us from making such a superficial judgment.

For, when it first makes an appearance in vision, the Lamb only "seems to have been slain." In the very next verse, he is identified as none other than "the lion of the tribe of Judah . . . who has conquered" (Rev 5:5–6). This visionary mixture of metaphors follows no narrative logic but poetically alludes to Jesus' death as ransoming "for God saints from every tribe and language, people and nation" (5:9). Even Jesus himself used the image of the Suffering Servant giving "his life as a ransom for the many" (Mark 10:45). But neither of these symbolic valuations of the unlikely result of the suffering of the just one refers to a literal, quasi-commercial transaction to win the loyalty of former pagans. They poetically allude to the universal impact of Jesus' triumph over death, not to his paying or being an actual ransom for anybody.

Clearly written to strengthen believers whom the author calls "the firstfruits of the human race for God and the Lamb" (14:4), Revelation's apocalyptic visions combine tragedy and triumph in a phantasmagoric mix. For those facing death at the hands of the "whore of Babylon," their martyrdom becomes a ticket to privileged status when the new Jerusalem is finally revealed. The combined images of sacrifice and martyrdom are offered as comfort for imperiled Christians ever since. But no martyrs ever suffered

Appendix A

death in ritual sacrifices; they suffered death through political/religious violence. Like the last becoming first, and the lowly and persecuted being blessed, the image of the triumphant Lamb reimagines a dark reality as the dawn of final salvation. The literary and religious artistry behind these metaphors rules out any of them literally describing God being offered or appeased by a bloody sacrifice on Calvary.

As a final note on the metaphorical substrate of the narrative underlying the Creed, I wish to press the point made above that metaphorical truth depends on literal falsity. What follows is a brief list of statements that bear the truth value of the overall story of paradox at the heart of our faith. Without understanding the "whispered no"[8] contained in all metaphorical affirmations, we end up not with paradox, but with contradictions, if not idolatries. For the story cannot be truthfully told without recognizing the following affirmations:

- God's temple is *not* made by hands
- Christ's priesthood is *not* earthly
- Christian sacrifices are *not* material
- grace is *nothing* but a gift
- spiritual wonders are *not* powers but gifts
- leaders in the community of believers are *not* to be tyrants but servants
- the poor are *not* cursed but blessed
- justice is *not* a matter of law
- sacrifice is *not* required but mercy is
- an enemy is *not* different from a neighbor
- being first is *not* to be served
- Jesus came *not* for the righteous but sinners
- those who withhold forgiveness are *not* forgiven

8. See above, chapter 3, n20, regarding Paul Ricoeur's theory of the "whispered no" in metaphor and symbol.

Appendix A

- being Peter is *not* a status but a mission
- the lowliest are *not* merely themselves but the king's
- the cross is *not* abandonment
- the Lord is *not* washed, but washes, and is *not* served but continues to serve the world
- his power and authority are *not* dominative, but ministerial
- for God is *not* a respecter of important persons.

Paradoxically, these seemingly negative affirmations liberate faith from descending into an ideological system of worldly religion. They redirect faith in the direction of mystery rather than mastery. Finally, they free us from pursuing our own justification, a need to justify ourselves and our endeavors, to prove ourselves right or righteous. They provide a framework for remaking the world in Christ's image, i.e., what the church praying the Creed must be about.

Bibliography

Abbott, Walter, ed. *The Documents of Vatican II*. New York: The America Press, 1966.
Alexander, Michelle. *The New Jim Crow: Mass Incarceration in the Age of Colorblindness*. Rev. ed. New York: New, 2012.
Alighieri, Dante. *The Divine Comedy 3: Paradise*. Baltimore: Penguin, 1964.
Armstrong, Karen. *The Case for God*. New York: Anchor, 2010.
Borg, Marcus. *The God We Never Knew: Beyond Dogmatic Religion to a More Authentic Contemporary Faith*. New York: HarperOne, 1997.
Boyarin, Daniel. *Intertextuality and the Reading of Midrash*. Bloomington: University of Indiana Press, 1991.
Jarvis, Brooke. "What Happens When You Breathe." *The New Yorker* (January 25, 2021) 65–67.
Cahill, Thomas. *Mysteries of the Middle Ages: The Rise of Feminism, Science, and Arts from the Cults of Catholic Europe*. The Hinges of History V. New York: Doubleday, 2006.
Catechism of the Catholic Church. Washington, DC: United States Catholic Conference, 1994.
Cullmann, Oscar. *Immortality of the Soul; or, Resurrection of the dead?: the witness of the New Testament*. Ingersoll Lecture. London: Epworth, 1955.
Denzinger, Heinrich, and Adolf Schönmetzer, eds. *Enchiridion Symbolorum, definitionum et declarationum de rebus fidei*. https://www.papalencyclicals.net/pius09/p9ineff.htm.
Dinter, Paul E. *Beyond Naïve Belief: The Bible and Adult Catholic Faith*. New York: Crossroad, 1994.
Edelman, Gerald M. *Wider Than the Sky: The Phenomenal Gift of Consciousness*. New Haven: Yale University Press, 2004.
Eliot, George. *Middlemarch: A Study of Provincial Life*. New York: Penguin, 2012.
Francis (pope). *Laudato Si'*. https://www.vatican.va/content/francesco/en/encyclicals/documents/papa-francesco_20150524_enciclica-laudato-si.html.
Goldblatt, Stephen. *The Swerve: How the World Became Modern*. New York: W. W. Norton, 2011.

Bibliography

Hart, David Bentley. *Atheist Delusions: The Christian Revolution and Its Fashionable Enemies*. New Haven: Yale University Press, 2009.
Haught, John F. *Deeper Than Darwin: The Prospect for Religion in the Age of Evolution*. Cambridge: Westview, 2003.
———. "Teilhard, Cosmic Purpose, and the Search for Extraterrestrial Intelligence." In *The Legacy of Pierre Teilhard de Chardin*, 9–23. Mahwah, NJ: Paulist, 2011.
Hinton, Anthony Ray. *The Sun Does Shine: How I Found Life and Freedom on Death Row*. With Lara Love Hardin. New York: St. Martin's, 2018.
Hopkins, Gerard Manley. *Poems of Gerard Manley Hopkins*. Memphis: General, 2010.
John XXIII (pope). *Pacem in Terris*. https://www.vatican.va/content/john-xxiii/en/encyclicals/documents/hf_j-xxiii_enc_11041963_pacem.html.
Ker, Ian. *John Henry Newman: A Biography*. Oxford Lives. New York: Oxford University Press, 1990.
Kimmerer, Robin Wall. *Braiding Sweetgrass: Indigenous Wisdom, Scientific Knowledge, and the Teaching of Plants*. Minneapolis: Milkweed, 2013.
Kushner, Harold S. *When Bad Things Happen to Good People*. New York: Anchor, 1981.
Lane, Belden C. "Spirituality and Political Commitment: Notes on a Liberation Theology of Non-Violence." *America* (March 14, 1981) 197–202.
Lewis, C. S. *The Pilgrim's Regress*. 3rd ed. Grand Rapids: Eerdmans, 1943.
"Matthew." *The Jewish Annotated New Testament*. Edited by Amy Levine and Mark Zvi Brettler. Oxford: Oxford University Press, 2011.
Mazzucato, Marianna. *Mission Economy: A Moonshot Guide to Changing Capitalism*. New York: Harper 2021.
Merton, Thomas, ed. *Gandhi on Non-Violence: A Selection of the Writing of Mahatma Gandhi*. New York: New Directions, 1965.
Mlodinow, Leonard. *The Drunkard's Walk: How Randomness Rules Our Lives*. New York: Pantheon, 2008.
Nussbaum, Martha C. *Political Emotions: Why Love Matters for Justice*. Cambridge: Harvard University Press, 2013.
O'Donohue, John. *Anam Cara: A Book of Celtic Wisdom*. New York: Harper Perennial, 2004.
Pascal, Blaise. *Pensées*. Translated by A. J. Krailsheimer. London: Penguin, 1995.
Patterson, Stephen J. *The Forgotten Creed: Christianity's Original Struggle against Bigotry, Slavery, and Sexism*. New York: Oxford University Press, 2018.
Prejean, Helen. *Dead Man Walking*. New York: Random House, 1995.
Ricoeur, Paul. "Biblical Hermeneutics." *Semeia* 4 (1975) 29–145.
Rohr, Richard. *The Divine Dance: The Trinity and Your Transformation*. New Kensington, PA: Whitaker House, 2016.
Sanders, E. P. *Jesus and Judaism*. Philadelphia: Fortress, 1985.
Sanders, James A. *Canon and Community: A Guide to Canonical Criticism*. Philadelphia: Fortress, 1984.

Bibliography

Shields, Jon A. "A Hard but Real Compromise Is Possible on Abortion." *The New York Times,* October 19, 2021. https://www.nytimes.com/2021/10/19/opinion/abortion-pro-life-movement.html.

Sternberg, Meir. *The Poetics of Biblical Narrative: Ideological Literature and the Drama of Reading.* Bloomington: Indiana University Press, 1987.

Stevenson, Bryan. *Just Mercy.* New York: One World, 2019.

Taylor, Charles. *A Secular Age.* Cambridge: Harvard University Press, 2007.

Van Wormer, Katherine S., and Lorenn Walker. *Restorative Justice Today: Practical Applications.* London: Sage, 2013.

Vermes, Geza. *Christian Beginnings: From Nazareth to Nicaea.* New Haven: Yale University Press.

Walden, Daniel. "Gender, Sex, and Other Nonsense." *Commonweal* 148 (2021) 22–26.

Weil, Simone. *Letter to a Priest.* Translated by A. F. Wills. 1951. New York: Routledge, 2002.

Wilson, Edward O. *The Social Conquest of Earth.* New York: W. W. Norton, 2012.

Wright, N. T. *Jesus and the Victory of God.* Christian Origins and the Question of God II. Minneapolis: Fortress, 1996.

www.ingramcontent.com/pod-product-compliance
Lightning Source LLC
Chambersburg PA
CBHW020856160426
43192CB00007B/953